P9-DNI-494

# Improve Your
# **Coaching &**
# **Training Skills**

# THE SUNDAY TIMES

CREATING SUCCESS

# Improve Your
# Coaching &
# Training Skills

## Patrick Forsyth

KOGAN
PAGE

London and Philadelphia

**Publisher's note**
Every possible effort has been made to ensure that the information contained in this book is accurate at the time of going to press, and the publishers and author cannot accept responsibility for any errors or omissions, however caused. No responsibility for loss or damage occasioned to any person acting, or refraining from action, as a result of the material in this publication can be accepted by the editor, the publisher or any of the authors.

First published in Great Britain and the United States in 2008 by Kogan Page Limited.

Apart from any fair dealing for the purposes of research or private study, or criticism or review, as permitted under the Copyright, Designs and Patents Act 1988, this publication may only be reproduced, stored or transmitted, in any form or by any means, with the prior permission in writing of the publishers, or in the case of reprographic reproduction in accordance with the terms and licences issued by the CLA. Enquiries concerning reproduction outside these terms should be sent to the publishers at the undermentioned addresses:

120 Pentonville Road
London  N1 9JN
United Kingdom
www.kogan-page.co.uk

525 South 4th Street, #241
Philadelphia  PA 19147
USA

© Patrick Forsyth, 2008

The right of Patrick Forsyth to be identified as the author of this work has been asserted by him in accordance with the Copyright, Designs and Patents Act 1988.

ISBN  978 0 7494 5235 3

The views expressed in this book are those of the author, and are not necessarily the same as those of Times Newspapers Ltd.

**British Library Cataloguing-in-Publication Data**

A CIP record for this book is available from the British Library.

**Library of Congress Cataloging-in-Publication Data**

Forsyth, Patrick.
  Improve your coaching and training skills / Patrick Forsyth.
    p. cm.
  ISBN 978-0-7494-5235-3
  1. Employees--Coaching of. 2. Employees--Training of. 3. Supervision of employees.
I. Title.
  HF5549.5.C53F67 2008
  658.3'124--dc22
                                                                2007044002

Typeset by Jean Cussons Typesetting, Diss, Norfolk
Printed and bound in India by Replika Press Pvt Ltd

Wisdom is not the exclusive possession of management.

*Akio Morita*

**PENDLETON PUBLIC LIBRARY**
**502 SW DORION AVE.**
**PENDLETON, OR 97801**       MAY       2008

# Contents

# Acknowledgements

Early in my career if anyone had suggested that I would ever do anything that involved writing or public speaking I would have dismissed the idea out of hand. Yet for most of my career I have made my living doing these two things.

I entered consultancy and training in a marketing role, but was soon persuaded to get involved in training – despite my reluctance. So, thanks are due to numbers of my consulting colleagues in those early days whose time, help and example showed me how training works, how to do it and how to do it effectively. Some of the same people, including the mentor mentioned in the text, also encouraged and helped me improve my writing.

These inputs, and my experience over some (well, all right then, many) years, have allowed me to write about training in this volume and do so in a way that can help others. The current book draws on an earlier title in this series, *Developing Your People*, written in 2000 and now out of print, and on an even earlier book *Running an Effective Training Session*, published by Gower back at the start of the 1990s.

Like so many others involved in training I have perhaps learnt most from the participants who have attended training programmes I have conducted over the years and around the world; thank you all. Your help, albeit mostly unwitting, is always invaluable.

*Patrick Forsyth*

# Preface

Sending men into war without training is like abandoning them.

*Confucius*

Managers have a tough job in the 21st century workplace. There is constant pressure to achieve results, yet constant distractions occur: too little of key resources including money and time, and a pace of change like never before in human history. Furthermore, the stage on which all this takes place is competitive and this fact too adds to the demands to succeed and to keep ahead. Probably management jobs were never easy, but these days they can be downright difficult. But managers have one key asset that makes undertaking their task easier. What is that?

*It's their people.*

Nothing allows a manager to achieve more than the fact of having a good team firing on all cylinders as it were. Or it should do. But this poses some questions. Are your team up to what you want them to do? And if so does this mean all of them, in every way, all the time? If they are honest, most managers will probably answer no to these questions. And if you do, then in today's organization you are normal. We all hope that most people can perform, as we want, and do so on most things, most of the time with appropriate self-sufficiency.

Sometimes, however, there may be a gap and routine matters are affected. Furthermore the pace of change is such that there will nearly always be some skills that must be extended and new skills that must be acquired.

And the responsibility for development, for 'people maintenance' or whatever you wish to call it, is – unequivocally – with line management.

## This book

So, the prime reader for this book is line managers: all those managing others and charged with maximizing their people's effectiveness (though it may assist anyone interested in or involved in training and development, including those new to that HR area). The book will:

▦ demonstrate the case for ongoing development;
▦ describe how it can positively influence results and staff motivation;
▦ review how to actually undertake development activity in key forms.

Initiating and implementing development in all its forms can involve a variety of methodologies and a number of different people in different parts of the organization. In a large organization some of the work can be delegated or subcontracted in some way and that is fine, though managers must brief others as necessary to make sure that so doing is effective.

Equally it may be, especially in a small organization, that if something is to be done, or done promptly, simply and cost-effectively, then the manager must do much or all of it unaided. Thus the book does not just review development as a process, it sets out information for implementing it, including how to actually conduct a training session (on the job or formal) if that is what you must do.

The emphasis is practical throughout. Training may in some senses be on a par with motherhood and apple pie – a 'good thing', but it is only truly at its best when it is well directed, effective and links directly to the job to be done and the results that must be achieved.

Good people and good performance – and hence good development – are fundamental to success in a fast changing and competitive world. Your organization's success – and that of you and your team - may depend, in part, on getting this right; hence this book.

Patrick Forsyth
Touchstone Training & Consultancy
28 Saltcote Maltings
Maldon
Essex CM9 4QP
patrick@touchstonetc.freeserve.co.uk
March 2008

# 1

# Development: route to success

'What a waste if I develop my staff and then they
leave.' To which the only logical response is: 'What
if you don't develop them – and they stay?'

*Apocryphal conversation*

Any manager will want the results that can be achieved from
development to make the time and effort it takes (for both
management and staff) worthwhile. There will always be
apparently good reasons not to act, or to delay. Just one is the
old chestnut quoted above.

As the 21st century gets under way, the job of management is
a challenging business. The job exists unequivocally to achieve
results. Whatever results a particular functional role may
dictate accrue – revenue, productivity, cost reduction and so on
– the pressures to achieve are often relentless. The busy
manager may feel so beset with problems that it is difficult to
call them challenges and to view them positively.

Certainly pressures have increased in recent years. There
never seems to be enough time or resources. There always
seems to be too much administration, paperwork and general
uncertainty and hassle. Probably no one works in a perfect
environment, or ever will, but any manager with a team of
people to manage has a significant antidote to all this – their
staff.

Results cannot usually be achieved by any single manager just 'doing it all themselves'. All the good things we want as managers – efficiency, effectiveness, productivity, creativity and ultimately results – are best achieved by the whole team working effectively, both as a team and as individuals. Thus everyone needs to be good at their own job. This of course means that they must be good at the individual tasks their job entails. These may be anything from conducting persuasive meetings with customers to interviewing job applicants or progressing complex projects, depending on the role of the job. Proficiency at the processes it involves along the way (eg, making decisions, report writing or time management) is also necessary. And nobody's perfect.

Despite the pressures of the 21st century workplace referred to in the Preface, development – and training its more formal partner – is essential if staff performance is to be maximized. Other things matter too, of course, motivation for example, which goes hand in hand with development in some ways. But development has a particular and a significant role to play. This is easy to say, and sounds essentially common sense – which it surely is. As the old saying has it: 'If you think training is expensive, try ignorance.' But the logic of its necessity does not automatically mean development will just happen. Nor does it make doing it easy. There are all too many potential difficulties:

■ lack of time;
■ inadequate resources;
■ under-funded training budgets;
■ conflicting priorities;
■ lack of clarity about what should be done;
■ failure to identify, or accept, the need;
■ shortfall in training skill or experience.

Any, or all, of the above (and more) can conspire to ensure that training and development do not occur. Or that they are done too little, too late or otherwise fudged. If proper staff development makes a difference (and this book certainly takes the view that it does) then the job of doing it and making it work must be tackled. Early on in this book the need for development and just what you can gain by good development policies and action are explained; so too as we go on are what is meant by good development and how it can be achieved.

Development may occur for many reasons, for example to:

■ enhance an individual's long-term career growth;
■ add or enhance skills needed in the short term;
■ fill a gap in past performance;
■ move an individual ahead or keep up with change.

Whatever the reason for it, and whatever its purpose, its execution must be approached in an appropriate way. This is, not least, because inappropriate action may do more harm than good, at worst failing to improve performance and acting to demotivate staff in the process.

Change alone (and the pace of change seems to accelerate as you watch; take IT as an example) provides ample reason to take an active view of the development process. The learning process needs to continue and all the skills that need deploying must keep pace.

So, you may say, I agree with all this – but that is what training departments are for, I have enough to do – let them provide what is needed. Perhaps they can; certainly in an organization of any size such a department will have a role to play.

But, to repeat, the responsibility to develop people resides *with the individual manager*. It is a responsibility that goes with the territory. If you have people reporting to you then you have to act to ensure that development takes place to establish, certainly to maintain, their ability to do a good job now and in the future. That need not mean the manager must personally provide all the development that takes place, but it *is* likely to mean he or she must initiate most of it (and maybe undertake some of it).

This book is intended to provide some practical guidance for managers wanting to exercise that responsibility, ensuring people, 1) are *able* to deliver, and undertake whatever is necessary to meet their objectives, and 2) *want* to produce the desired performance. Development is crucial to the first, motivation to the second and, as we will see, these two must go hand in hand.

Before continuing, consider what development can do. Essentially there are three things; it can:

1. impart knowledge;
2. develop skills;
3. change attitudes.

Sometimes it must do all three together, though the timescales may vary and, as a general rule, it takes longer to change attitudes – especially long-held ones – than to get new facts across. The purposes of any sort of development may vary widely. It may be to:

■ extend knowledge;
■ introduce new skills, adding to the range available in an individual or a group;
■ fine-tune existing skills, producing a greater level of performance in the future;
■ prompt fresh thinking and ideas, and play a part in evolving new ways of doing things.

Development may be intended to have an immediate effect or initiate a radical change longer term. Its relationship with targets and the results people may be charged with achieving may be close, or it may be that a more general effect is intended. In addition, just to make the span of influence clear, it may be linked to a host of other factors such as:

■ changing organization structure;
■ decentralization or links around an organization with multiple locations;
■ technological change;
■ change in business practice, policy or culture;
■ market and competitive change.

Development should always make a difference; a positive difference that helps make an organization stronger, more effective and better able to cope with the challenging environment in which it doubtless must operate. Again the potential results of training are many. They include, for example:

■ extended staff retention;
■ increased job flexibility;
■ competitive advantage;
■ faster response to events;
■ improved motivation (and lower incidence of absence and accidents).

So, development is necessary. Its execution is worthwhile and, like any management task, must be done in a way that maximizes the results from the time and effort involved. It does not just happen, of course, it does take time – though one of the objectives of this book is to show that any manager can do a great deal with even modest time and money.

So with these positive thoughts in mind, how do people view development?

# Staff attitudes

In many organizations there is a general sense of approval about development. How much training is done certainly varies over time, though training should be an investment and a continuous process. If this is the feeling throughout an organization, and if it is backed by appropriate resources, including a suitable budget, then it should make it easier to ensure that the development activity that follows makes a difference.

In this context, how is an individual likely to feel? What, in fact, do members of your own staff, or team, think? First, consider how they are likely to view their job and the way it is supervised. To do so in detail involves the theory and process of motivation and a detailed description of this is beyond my brief here (if you want chapter and verse see my book *How to Motivate People* in this same series). Suffice to say that both the things that motivate and those that do the reverse can all be usefully linked to development.

Although there can be exceptions (being sent on a course because of some fault or failure, perhaps), your staff are certainly likely to regard training and development as something desirable, indeed even as essential. One thing that always reminds me of this, and highlights the implications for management, is the many surveys I have seen, asking people to list in order of desirability the characteristics that they would like to have in the 'perfect' manager. Many factors are always listed: managers should be fair, good listeners, skilled at their own job, decisive, and more.

One factor, however, consistently comes at or near the top of such a list. People say, 'I want to work with a manager from whom I learn.' Further questioning reveals that this is seen in two ways. First, learning direct from their contact with the manager; secondly, learning from the development that a manager organizes for them (for example, arranging attendance on a course). This becomes even more important in a workplace environment that is now frankly competitive; the concept of jobs for life is as dead as the dinosaurs and many people see working at what is called 'active career management' as essential.

The lesson could not be clearer. Development may be good – necessary – for all sorts of reasons, but always because people want and enjoy it. The manager who ignores the development of his or her staff, or is seen to treat it as of no great consequence, is likely to have problems.

A final point here: actually using development as an incentive – 'If you do so and so, I will send you on that course you want to attend' – needs care. On the one hand you might link training activities, making completing some simple form of development, a prerequisite for attending a course. On the other, linking attendance to the achievement of some unrelated target might make it seem that development is not really important. It might seem so if it appears that the development is not something that *should* be done, rather that it is something it might be nice to do. A careful balance is necessary here.

# A development culture

At this stage, having said something about why every manager should take a positive view of training, the wider aspects of the view taken within and around an organization must be considered. It obviously helps if *everyone* in the organization feels development is necessary and important. As has been said, this feeling will, in all likelihood, exist – people want personal development. It will be more in evidence if people believe that the organization has a genuine culture of development. The two things reinforce one another.

A positive development culture will help ensure people:

■ take training and development seriously;
■ give the necessary time to it;
■ play a part in identifying what should be done (and how);
■ work at learning from it and use new skills appropriately.

This process must be fostered on a continuing basis. In other words, eyes must be kept on the training ball if it is to be built into ongoing operations in a way that maximizes the results it brings. How is this done? In a word: through *communication*.

There are a variety of ways in which a manager can influence the activity of an organization and provide opportunities to build a development culture. This can happen, for example, through:

■ staff job appraisal procedures;
■ internal communication (from memo to e-mail);
■ newsletters and notice boards (electronic and physical);
■ training rooms, resources and libraries;
■ feedback procedures (eg, debriefings and course evaluation forms);
■ staff and departmental meetings;
■ annual reports (and other annual reporting procedures).

Together all these and more provide opportunity to engage in a dialogue – a process of communication that continually mentions training. Here the case for training can be made, the results of training reported and new training initiatives planned and flagged. It can be a two-way process, canvassing ideas and suggestions as much as reporting what goes on.

Every manager can usefully play a part in such a process. You need to watch for opportunities; indeed perhaps you need to actively plan to take an ongoing initiative. These things are helped in a powerful way if there is a commitment from the top of the organization. If you are lucky senior managers in your own organization will champion the development cause. If this does not happen, you may need to direct communication to these levels to influence matters.

# The range of development methods

If you are reading this book, then you are by definition involved to some extent in an element of development activity.

Self-development is part of the overall process. Similarly, if you let someone else read it – or, as a manager, recommend or insist on it – you are contributing to the development of others. Actually, hang onto your copy and get them to buy their own, every little royalty helps and ... but I digress.

The point is, first, that development encompasses some very simple methodology. None the worse for that – sometimes the simple approach can be highly effective. Secondly, the escalation from the simplest can take in a whole range of things. Some are still essentially simple. For example, let us go back to reading a book. You can read it, you can pass it to others, or you can link it to some sort of system (circulating a list of recommended reading). You can continue increasing complexity in this way. Add a target (everyone must read a book each month or quarter). Add feedback (what we have learnt from this month's book to be discussed at a staff meeting). Or add a project (read *How to Write Reports and Proposals*, another title in this series, telling your people to discuss the next report they write with you to see how their style may have adapted and improved). There are a good many options and methods ranged between this sort of thing and something at the other end of the scale: someone attending a three-month course at a US business school, for instance.

As well as training methods, the various techniques of training, for example role-playing or other exercises that can be used on a course or have a training role in isolation, must be considered. The range of possibilities is enormous. At one end we have a group taken out of operational activity for a long period (perhaps many weeks or months) to attend a course. At the other we have the simple reading of an appropriate book.

Always the role of the individual line manager is key. Progressively we now look at various aspects of what must be done and how to go about it. The returns can be substantial – a considered approach that does a good job of undertaking the development part of any manager's responsibilities is very worthwhile.

Your attitude and action with regard to development can literally make the difference between success and failure. You need to see the objective as development designed to achieve excellence in your team. The management fear, quoted at the start of this chapter, of people being trained who then leave to go elsewhere, needs to be addressed. People will leave; occasionally it is just inevitable. How much worse, however, to manage a group of people so mediocre that none of them is sufficiently competent to *be able* to get another job. Better to aim to train them to work effectively and motivate them to want to continue doing so.

# 2

# Development and management responsibility

> A manager develops people. He directs people
> or he misdirects. He brings out what is in them,
> or he stifles them.
>
> *Peter Drucker*

First in this chapter, let's put development in the context of day-to-day operations. Whatever the nature of any job, its existence and its working are usually organized and supported by some element of formality. This is necessary if what needs to be done is to be done effectively. The nature of that formality is perhaps best considered if we look at a new situation.

Imagine a growing organization. In a particular department, work volume demands that the number of staff employed be increased. Just pulling in the first person that chances along and saying 'fill the gap' cannot do this. Recruitment and selection processes must be conducted carefully and demand a systematic approach. Many people find the processes involved, including what may sometimes seem like endless interviews, a chore. Worse, they assume they have a God-given ability to assess people 'as they walk through the door', as some say. Such a combination of attitudes can be disastrous.

Good recruitment is an essential prerequisite to ensuring that a team functions well. Getting it wrong has dire consequences: certainly the time and cost of getting rid of a candidate who should never have been appointed in the first place, and the dilution of effectiveness (at worst, damage) they may have while in office. It is always worth the time and trouble necessary to make the best appointments possible. Some of the formalities that help are also useful as you move on to consider how to develop any employee who you are happy to retain.

These include a *job definition:* a clear statement of what a particular job entails, spelling out the objectives, responsibilities and the tasks to be undertaken; certainly without thinking this through sensible recruitment is impossible. To complete this picture, there is a *candidate profile:* a matching and clear statement of the kind of person required to do the job (experience, knowledge, qualifications, background, capabilities etc).

Such may be sufficient to aid the recruitment and selection process. They help produce any necessary job advertisements (or agency briefings), help focus interviews and guide the final selection.

Beyond that, other things may be necessary. For instance, a *job description*: this goes beyond the job definition. It is often more formal and in many organizations links to Personnel Department or Human Resources systems that may demand standard documentation around the organization. (*Note:* it may also need to be constructed to link appropriately to employment legislation – always a consideration for any manager – so that it spells out objectives, standards and such like.)

The job description may be regarded as having two distinct roles: 1) a formal one (linked to personnel systems, appraisal, etc); and 2) an informal one, providing a *working* reference, a document that acts, day to day, to help ensure that the correct focus is maintained both in the job and around an organization or department.

It is good practice to ensure that job descriptions are copied to any group of people whose work overlaps or interrelates in any way. Mary should see Ron's and Ron should see Mary's, and so on. This should include some crossing of levels, so that if you manage other people you should make sure that they see your job description – how else will they fully appreciate the relationship between what each of you does? If necessary this may mean preparing a cut down version of job descriptions, editing them to remove any confidential information (for example about salary or employment grades).

# The link with development

Such systems form the foundation to the manager's ability not only to manage, but also to develop people. It is clearly essential to have a clear, and commonly agreed, view of what a particular job entails before you can look at a person's ability to carry out their responsibilities, and whether training of some sort is necessary or would help them perform better.

Objectives, for example, must be clear; and it is worth a small digression to spell out just what that means.

## Job objectives

Objectives should focus attention and effort on the precise nature of the activity required. If objectives are stated too generally, then they will provide inadequate description and – at worst – they will indicate no direction. Saying that the job of a Customer Relations Executive is to 'liaise with customers' is no more than a glimpse of the obvious; as such it provides little practical help either to the holder of such a job or to their manager.

Objectives must be:

Specific
Measurable
Achievable
Realistic
Timed

Many refer to this as making objectives SMART, using the initial letters of the words above. Being *specific* and *measurable* go together, and often mean putting some numbers against the objective: in the case of the job mentioned above, maybe 'to handle 100 customer telephone calls a day'. This can be extended, for instance to add more quantitative information such as 'with 70 per cent of calls resulting in an order' – or specifying the nature and minimum value of the orders.

*Achievable* means that it can be done (500 calls in a day might be beyond anyone; the number selected could be picked to stretch people, but must be possible). *Realistic* means desirable, something from which the organization will benefit. For example, it would not be realistic to keep customers on the telephone for too long; even if they enjoy a chat it is not productive (so again numbers could be added and made to reflect factors of this sort).

*Timing* is always important, and it may be necessary to link this to other standards in a variety of ways. Here, for instance, timing could encompass daily activity through to annual achievement and also to output: 'resolving all complaints within 24 hours', perhaps.

# Creating a development plan

A development plan may be necessary for the whole organization. Drawn up by the HR department, or by consultants, it should reflect the requirements of individual parts of the organization (managers must be consulted). It can then help plan and chart progress across the whole organization. This does not in any way absolve the individual manager from the responsibility of having an agreed plan for each and every individual working in his or her team. This plan need not be complex, but why is it necessary?

First, it is necessary because even with a modest number of people reporting to you it is not possible to commit everything to memory (you surely have enough day to day, operational matters to concern yourself with). Secondly, because it bestows importance on the whole area of development, as it does on the plan for each person. Seeing that their training plan is the subject of some concern to you, will motivate people.

More of individual development plans anon. Ahead of that, because development plans are, most often, an extension of the job appraisal process, a word about that is appropriate here too.

## Job appraisal

Like recruitment, this is an area some (many?) managers find awkward or distasteful. It is only so if the system that is being used is inappropriate, or perhaps if the reasons for it, or the way to undertake it, are not fully explained or appreciated.

In fact, appraisal is a real opportunity – for manager and staff alike, and sound training and development plans are inextricably linked with it. It is difficult to imagine development running well alongside an inadequate appraisal process. If your staff do not see appraisal in the right light, it is no good blaming central departments or processes – the responsibility is yours (though perhaps you should be assisted by others in the organization in the task of explaining). Consider for a moment: what exactly are job appraisals for?

Put simply, past performance is reviewed through appraisal in order to help make future performance better. It is an ongoing process, of course, and the (often annual) appraisal is only the most formal manifestation of it. As a manager, your performance (and perhaps the outcome of your own job appraisal too!) is dependent upon your team performing well. Appraisal is a prime opportunity to help secure that future performance.

Specifically, the purpose of appraisal meetings is to:

■ review individuals' past performance;
■ plan their future work and role;
■ set specific individual goals for the future;
■ agree and create individual ownership of such goals;
■ identify development needs and set up development activity;
■ carry out on-the-spot coaching;
■ obtain feedback;
■ reinforce or extend reporting relationships;
■ act as a catalyst to delegation;
■ focus on long-term career progression;
■ motivate.

The above, a list you could maybe add to, are not mutually exclusive. Appraisals are usually trying to address a number of different things, but development should always rank high among them.

This is not the place to review the whole process of appraisal, but with an eye on development you should certainly take on board certain key approaches. You need to:

■ ensure your people understand what appraisal is for, not least how it can help them;
■ encourage them to prepare for appraisal and aim to get the most out of it (this means not just having a think before the meeting, but running an 'appraisals file', collecting information and documents through the year – a year is, after all, a long period to recall – and considering

progressively what the events of the year mean for appraisal);

■ set a clear agenda, and issue it ahead of the meeting (maybe in consultation with the appraisee) and make clear the importance of developmental issues;

■ encourage appraisees to talk (after all, it is them you are trying to find out about – they should hold the floor as it were for more than 50 per cent of the time, during which your job is to listen);

■ focus on the future. A constructive appraisal is not an opportunity to lay blame (well, this may be appropriate sometimes), but to plan for the future, picking up both positive and negative events and linking them to the future. More than 50 per cent of the discussion should look ahead – maybe much more.

In this way you can ensure that the meeting will be useful and it will be seen as useful, before, during and after it is held. Always bear in mind that people are not only concerned about their progress, they will want to get the best from appraisals. There is plenty of guidance on this (for example my own book, *Appraising Job Performance*, from How to Books, is a case in point), and you should ensure people's expectations are met.

# The development dimension

Discussion of development should be a key part of the appraisal meeting. Several factors need addressing.

## Identifying development needs

This is clearly the first stage. It stems both from the activity of the year immediately past and from further back. A project which the appraisee executed during the year may have highlighted something that needs attention: a skills deficiency of some sort perhaps.

## Agreeing development needs

It is not enough for a manager simply to say, 'You need training.' The individual must recognize both the weakness (or gap; it may be something in which he or she never needed to have competence in the past), and agree the need to correct it.

## Discussing suitable action to correct the situation

This might be linked to an agreed decision – 'So, you attend the next course on that' – or to future action (beyond the appraisal meeting) —'Let's find out what sort of course would suit and talk about it again in a month or so.' Action must be specific here, making clear who will do what and setting deadlines (and sometimes budgets).

## Taking action now

Time will forbid all but the most straightforward things being addressed within the appraisal meeting itself, but sometimes a brief word is all that is necessary.

## Recording conclusions and linking to an action plan

Development action must not be forgotten (even in the heat of operational pressures), so clear notes need to be made. Matters may have to be summarized in the overall report that often follows appraisal meetings. An *action* note is important too, however. A memo, or e-mail, to the appraisee can confirm matters. Moreover the manager needs a personal note to act as a reminder. This can take many forms: for instance a diary note (electronic or otherwise). The importance of development prompts many managers to keep a current record sheet (this could be a page for each person they manage in a system such as Filofax, or a format on screen in a computer system or electronic personal organizer).

The record – which effectively forms the individual development plan referred to earlier – will have three dimensions of development to note. First, it should list the needs identified (for example: *skills of formal presentation* must be strengthened). Then it should list the action agreed (*attending a course*, though this could well be preceded or followed by other action). Thirdly it should note – and link to the diary – any ongoing review, consultation or coaching sessions that are necessary between manager and subordinate (or indeed that will involve anyone else).

This kind of record can show the state of play at any particular moment. It can be updated, amended or extended as required (or as agreed by both parties) and act as a catalyst, ensuring that action follows the formal appraisal meeting and that what needs to be done – both immediately afterwards and in the longer term – does actually occur.

Thus the record and the appraisal, and the other communications they prompt, combine to produce a rolling plan that creates the continuous focus on the development that is needed. Working in this kind of way also guarantees that things will not be forgotten as doing so will appear as a lack of interest in, or commitment to, the member of staff concerned. If this is felt, then what may well start as enthusiasm can quickly deteriorate into disappointment and disillusionment, which reduces motivation and dilutes performance.

# A cycle of improvement

Thus managers have a responsibility to address the question of performance in the job of everyone reporting to them, and to continue doing so over time. In the first place it is important to define the job and select someone truly suitable to fill it. Then the performance has to be regularly reviewed, and the job appraisal process puts a formality on this. Implementing the plan that stems from this activity is an ongoing process. It needs to be set up in a way that focuses attention on it, and linked to systems that make it happen.

Level of competence is not something to be addressed once in a while in an ad hoc way. Creating it and maintaining it is at the heart of any manager's job, so next we consider what that implies in terms of action.

# 3

# The development task

*The eggs do not teach the hen.*

*Russian proverb*

It has been said already that training and development should be a continuous process. Earlier we looked at recruitment as a starting point to this process, at the way in which formalities such as job descriptions help, and at the overall role of job appraisal. Here we look more at the day-to-day job of development and the ways of accurately identifying where exactly development must be directed.

The manager's job is to ensure the right performance from others, those reporting to him or her, and to make sure this is maintained. Realistically, both what people do and how they do it varies over time. Sometimes this has nothing to do with their level of skills and overall competence; people do more or less because of a variety of factors, and other influences, from organization to motivation, are instrumental in controlling this. People's actual ability to do their job is key however, and this needs constant monitoring.

# The development gap

In one sense any development may be regarded as a 'good thing'. Indeed, it should after all do good. In addition, as we will see, some training and development may be unspecific and have general, long-term aims; and be none the less appropriate for that. But there is a need in most organizations to look at the current situation and the short term, and to use development to help achieve aims that stem from business plans describing the next period (whatever that may be defined as being in an organization). The process of looking at this, and deciding what needs to be done can be tackled systematically, as follows.

## Examine job descriptions

This allows you to review the levels of knowledge and skills that a particular job demands, and the attitudes required of the person who may do it. This states the ideal and the current position and is not, at this stage, linked to the individual currently doing the job.

## Examine the person

This enables you to look, alongside the ideal, at what the situation actually is currently. How do the knowledge, skills and attitudes of the individual stack up alongside what the job demands? This information comes from observation of the person, his or her performance and results. Formal appraisal is a key part of this, as is – as we will see – other, less formal, evaluation.

## Look to the future

Before reaching any conclusions from the process described so far, you need also to think ahead, again focusing on the job.

What will the job demand in future that will be different from the current situation? What developments (in the organization, in technology, in the market and expectation of customers – and more) are coming? Specifically, what new skills, knowledge or attitudes will then be necessary, and how will existing ones need to change?

## Defining the gap

Together, two factors coming from the above may define a gap: the combination of any shortfall in current levels of competence plus the need to add to this in future. This is the so-called training (or development) 'gap' and gives you the area towards which development must be directed with any individual.

Of course, the picture produced may be fine; no immediate action may be necessary. The reality is most likely that some action – major or minor – is necessary. If so you need a plan of action to deal with implementation. Again, viewing this systematically provides a simple checklist approach as to what to do:

- ■ *List what needs to be addressed:* whatever is identified, .from minor matters that need only a small input to new skills that must be approached from square one.
- ■ *Rate the list in terms of priorities:* in most organizations resources (time, money and training facilities) are finite. It is unlikely to be possible to do everything that might be desirable instantly, and impossible to select what comes first or should be postponed without some clear thinking through of priorities.
- ■ *Put some timing to it:* having established priorities you need to consider when things are to be done. What is urgent? What can be postponed without causing problems and what might be addressed in parts? (Perhaps with some-

thing being done early on, but action also planned to follow up and complete the training task later.)

■ *Consider the most suitable method:* this needs to relate quite closely to timing. With a list of desirable training and priorities set, you need to consider exactly how something will be approached (a course, a project, whatever).

■ *Calculate costs:* this is always an important issue, and may involve some compromise and balancing of different approaches (more people given some training versus fewer people given thorough training, for example).

■ *Link to an action plan:* the net result of these deliberations needs to be documented, and turned into a rolling plan that sets out what will be done, in what way, when and who will be involved. This may be recorded in part on a per person basis as suggested earlier.

In this way training and development activities can be considered, worked out and scheduled on a basis that makes sense. Such consideration must:

■ relate closely to operational matters;
■ link and liaise as necessary with any appropriate central department or manager (eg, a training manager) – not least to draw on their experience and expertise;
■ reflect suitable consultation with the staff involved, a process that stems originally from job appraisal discussions.

To make such a process possible presupposes knowing enough about the people concerned and their performance; this, in turn, presupposes some evaluation throughout the year.

# Evaluating throughout the year

Appraisal is a formal process. It was mentioned earlier and is likely to happen, on at least an annual basis, in any organization of any size (employment legislation alone in the UK has exerted considerable pressure for this to be so). However, most managers would concede that they would know precious little about their staff if that was the only occasion during the year on which their performance was discussed.

Other occasions for evaluation need to be found, and a basis for using them effectively worked out. Some of these will be very informal and need no documenting here. Others will be incorporated into occasions that exist primarily for other purposes, such as departmental or project meetings.

Some should be specifically for the purpose of evaluation. To be able to do this you need to be sure that there is:

■ a common understanding of the job in question (this is one of the rationales for the formality of job descriptions and for their being regarded as working documents) so that the detail can be discussed;
■ similar understanding of any targets involved;
■ such understanding reflected in an agreed system for evaluation.

If this is the case then discussion about the job can flow easily. Such discussion is often best preceded by observation; you need to look not only at *what* is being achieved, but *how* it is being done. The latter is the only way of linking to skills and techniques and seeing how they are being deployed. Remember that simply looking at results, for example the number of things done or something that is recorded, does not tell you *how* things were done or, of itself, show a possibility of change and improvement.

Practice varies in exactly how such evaluation sessions are conducted. Some managers favour a very informal approach, others something more formal and fully documented. What is important is that there is a continuum of activity. Some action may consist of no more than a few words in passing, while some will be short sessions maybe linking an element of evaluation to projects or other discussions. On other occasions a dedicated session will focus exclusively on evaluation.

Even if you opt for the informal, the way the session might be documented makes its precise nature clear. There are two elements to have in mind during evaluation.

## 1. The activities that the job entails

Here you need to tease things out so that *all* the constituent elements of a job are 'on the table' as it were. Consider someone dealing with customers on the telephone. If they are handling a complaint, say, they need a good telephone manner. This in turn necessitates a whole list of things being done right: they have to be polite, get the burden of the complaint clear, appear sympathetic to give confidence, calm down people who are angry and more – much more. Their effectiveness is dependent on the totality of this. Individual elements are important, and weakness in one may well dilute the effectiveness of the whole.

Evaluation needs to look at *how* these things are being done. It is insufficient just to say that on the whole customers are happy with how they are dealt with; to deal with any weakness you have to be clear why it is occurring, perhaps in this case because of poor listening skills. Similarly, the *why* is just as important if you are to build on strengths. Let me emphasize this last point. Evaluating should be as much about building on strengths as identifying and correcting weaknesses. This is a factor that helps create acceptability for the whole process.

The relationship with job descriptions is clear and they may form the starting point for such a list, though for evaluation purposes more detail may be necessary. The point is that both manager and staff need to be clear precisely what it is that is being evaluated.

# 2. The level of performance

Here you need some sort of scale on which to mark people. This kind of thing often exists in formal appraisal documentation; indeed that may help produce what you need here. Simplicity is the key. You need a rating scale. An even number of ratings is best (avoiding the temptation to mark down the middle too much), perhaps four or six levels. This might be stated as *satisfactory, above average, below average,* and *unsatisfactory.* The words are largely unimportant. You might equally use a scale of 1, 2, 3 and 4 (as long as everyone is clear which end is which!). On the other hand, sometimes you may want to put a description to the ratings: for instance that someone always does something, nearly always does it and so on.

The marking here is not something that needs to be completed comprehensively every time. With a long list of factors this might not even be practical. So different things may need addressing on different occasions. Nor is it a system the results of which need to sit forever on the record. It is simply a spur to action.

Imagine four rating scales: there is effectively a line down the middle. Marking on the top two might be taken to mean 'no action', though there might be something to say about either. Marking on the lower two means performance is such that remedial action is necessary, especially on the lowest – and this prompting of action is what you are after. Evaluation prompts a constructive dialogue about performance, and the rating element of it prompts action if and where necessary.

Many managers implement this sort of activity with no actual completion of a form (though a checklist might help). Certainly many would say that, beyond a reminder of action to follow, any documentation that is used should not be kept on the record, though some factors may need noting separately on an individual's file.

Overall, the intention is to prompt and channel constructive dialogue aimed at fine-tuning performance, and to do so in a way that is acceptable and effective. It is an opportunity to motivate when things go well, or are made to do so following action. It links to straightforward counselling and on-the-job training (more of which later). And it can link to formal development activity too.

Regular inputs of this sort need not be disproportionately time-consuming and, effectively done, can pay dividends in terms of improved performance.

# The effect on the individual

The key to making evaluation work is that it is a practical process. First, people must understand the job they are employed to undertake and, in detail, what needs to be done to enable them to make that job effective – both of which they certainly should.

Secondly, they must see the need for good performance and thus the need to ensure it happens. Then they must find useful the process of evaluation and its link with developmental activity, whether simple or more elaborate. If the discussions it prompts are fair, constructive and, above all, *if people find it helps them* (maybe making the job easier or more satisfying) then the process will be accepted. More than that, the existence of such activity will be found motivational.

Managers must set it up, explain and undertake it in the right way. If it is made effective then it can become a regular, inherent element of the management process – one that builds on strengths, nips weaknesses in the bud and fine-tunes performance on a continuing basis.

There is one more advantage to all this which, at the end of the day, is perhaps more important than anything else – creating the right habit.

# Creating the right habit

How is it some people excel at what they do? There are probably many reasons (including their willingness to take advantage of help given, as we have been discussing). One reason in
particular is paramount. It is the ability of someone to undertake self-analysis linked to fine-tuning. People who understand
what they have to do and what makes it work well, and who
*consider what they do and how they can improve it still more*
will always have a head start on those who just go through the
motions.

Some people have this habit of thinking about what they do.
They handle a customer complaint, or whatever, and say to
themselves afterwards: How did that go? What might I have
done differently? What must I keep in mind for next time? And
so on. It makes a difference – they resolve to act differently in
future and do so. This sort of conscious self-analysis is invaluable. Done on a regular basis – and we may only be talking
about a few seconds thought sometimes – it can lead to resolve
and action that progressively builds performance, and does so
regularly, and *on a self-contained basis*, without a prompt from
a manager.

A manager's work with people can certainly act to improve
performance, and will do so if it is well executed. But you are
not at people's elbow every moment of the day. The result that
will influence performance most, therefore, is the way in which
such activity can act to develop such a habit in people; a practice that allows them to evaluate and improve their own performance in the manager's absence. What you do with people in
evaluation, and the action that follows it, can be used to install
such a habit – and that is perhaps its most valuable result.

Of course, training can take many forms. One job is to assess
methods; usually a mix of things can be used and works best –
from the quick and simple to the more complex; see the box
below.

# Training and development methods

There are so many ways of achieving the learning and change of behaviour that are desired in most organizations. Some are simple, ranging from an exchange of words to the reading of a book. Others include:

- on-the-job counselling;
- courses: internal and external, long and short;
- a session using a training film;
- role-playing;
- management games and simulations;
- 'packaged' training: a plethora of 'kits' using pre-prepared materials of all sorts (often on computer);
- open learning;
- internet-based courses;
- training linked to professional qualifications;
- brainstorming and creative circles;
- the use of resource centres;
- job rotation and job swaps;
- mentoring;
- secondment (sometimes outside the organization);
- sabbaticals (the organizational gap year with a learning dimension).

All have their place, often in sequence with one thing leading to another, and must match the job to be done without either skimping it or over-engineering the process.

Some of the methods in the selection listed above form part of our coverage here; others are beyond the brief. The main focus from here on is on the manager and what he or she can put over personally either through on-the-job coaching, investigated in the next chapter, or in more formal training sessions or courses.

At this point let us be clear: development is dependent on a thorough understanding of what must be done – no one can improve performance if they are uncertain of what it is or precisely how it is produced. With a firm factual basis for enhancing performance, refreshed as it were by regular evaluation, and ultimately by self-evaluation, and with an acceptance that development should take place – it can be made to happen.

# 4

# On-the-job coaching

Knowledge advances by steps, and not by
leaps.

*Lord Macaulay*

Before we get on to anything more formal, there is one way of
going about development that can be usefully used on an
ongoing basis and which fits in neatly with everyday operations. The phrase 'on-the job training' implies a range of
activity, ways of working with a member of your staff that can
be integrated into the day-to-day activity of you both. It is at
once largely low key and highly effective. Like so much else in
management, however, its effectiveness can easily be diluted by
an ad hoc approach, and this chapter is designed to set out
something of the systematic approach that can make it work
best.

This aspect of development is something that is personally
applied. You have control, and the effect is immediate. This is
thus something that is an inherent part of the manager/subordi-
nate relationship. It should strengthen this, have a positive
motivational effect and – of course above all – act to improve
performance.

# The beneficiaries of on-the-job coaching

It is worth considering two different categories of people: new, and existing (and more experienced) staff. Let's consider these in turn:

## New staff

Here on-the-job coaching is part of the induction process. Clearly it is important when people are first appointed that they understand the job, and are able to undertake all the various activities that make it up. With internal appointments, less briefing may be necessary, though you should not automatically assume that the knowledge and skill someone gleaned in another department is exactly what he or she will need while working for you.

More so with external appointments: people may have a skill but be used to applying it in a rather different way from what is now necessary. For example, someone dealing with people on the telephone may have good telephone skills but be used only to dispensing information. If a new job demands, say, offering advice, then skills may need some adaptation. Such transitions may not be complicated, but they need to be dealt with and dealt with promptly and certainly.

At an early stage in someone's work with you there are a number of ways in which your input to his or her development can be beneficial. These include helping in:

■ establishing skills on the right basis as a foundation of the way someone will work during his or her tenure in a particular job;
■ developing good working habits, which in turn act to produce consistency of performance;

■ producing attitudes to, and understanding of, what needs to be done so that a person is inherently likely to be more self-sufficient in what he or she does;

■ establishing an attention to detail, for example in following prescribed systems, that make for precision of work in whatever way is required;

■ building confidence quickly in what he or she does and in a way that effects his or her ability to work effectively.

All such intentions can be important, and if new employees are set up right, so to speak, they will be better able to operate as is required thereafter. Attitude and activity go together. For instance, if you want someone to adopt a creative approach, to think about what goes on and how it might be improved, rather than simply follow a slavish pattern, then this is best established early on.

## Experienced staff

Here the requirement is rather different. Even when performance is good, there is a need to fine-tune skills, and to add them. There is also a need for briefing to continue as policy and practice change over time. This – coupled with the sensible attitude that even the best performance can be improved – means that development, certainly in many things, never stops. Yet experienced people can easily resent training, seeing some of it at least as a negative reflection on their current skills. Good on-the-job coaching, and indeed the routine of its use, can make ongoing development acceptable and thus, in turn, allow it to have a more certain effect.

Where training and development in specific skills are involved there is a need to consider carefully exactly what is needed.

# Defining the development task

Whatever is being contemplated, your view of it must be clear. Specifically, this means defining clearly the following points.

## What the individual must be able to do

Or – let us be necessarily pedantic – *exactly* what he or she has to do and how he or she should go about it. Sometimes this means learning to follow an exact procedure; alternatively it might mean adopting a less rigid, but specific approach. It could mean both. Someone who must handle complaints, for instance, must deal with them systematically (if certain things are not done in a certain order it may well make what can be a difficult situation worse). But he or she must also deal with them in a way that is tailored to the individual complainant; indeed anything less can make it seem that no individual concern is being expressed, and it seems as if 'this is how they deal with it to fob us off'.

## The conditions under which performance must be achieved

On-the-job coaching must reflect the real world. It is no good people being able to do something right only in highly artificial conditions; they must be able to do it as it needs to be done. Consider a specific example. I am involved in a good deal of sales training. Sales people need to be able to communicate persuasively (and do more besides, but let's keep it simple). They not only need to be able to communicate in this way, but to do so in a meeting or contact of appropriate duration. Sometimes this time can be very short. In the world of pharmaceuticals, sales people calling on doctors must often do so amongst their appointments with patients. In a meeting designed to inform and update a doctor about their drugs (what in the industry is referred to as *detailing*) they have – in the UK at least – an average of around four minutes to do so. Someone who is wonderfully persuasive – eventually – simply cannot do the job. The short duration is a 'given'. Operating that way goes with the territory as they say, and subsequently any training directed at this area must reflect that reality. Any job doubtless has such factors associated with it.

## The link with standards

The duration of sales visits referred to above may always be short, but it is not an exact duration. Sometimes there is an exact precision that must be reflected in work and training alike and this links to targets or standards that form part of the job description. So, for example, standards specifying the number of customer calls to be handled, on average, in the call centres so beloved of our financial institutions these days, have a mandatory impact on the job – and on development undertaken to equip people to do it.

Thus, development can best proceed with clear thinking in these sorts of ways and always with clear objectives resulting from them. Given a discreet on-the-job development objective, what is then necessary is a systematic way of approaching it.

# A systematic approach

To be effective, and to get things done productively because time is always of the essence, it is best to approach things systematically. Taking things from scratch, for most tasks the following approach makes good sense.

## 1. Describe the task

The first step is to tell people what needs to be done. Normally this means what it says: telling them verbally, though description could be enhanced in other ways, ranging from a checklist in a manual to a tutorial on a computer screen.

## 2. Demonstrate what must be done

This is designed to reinforce description and help ensure that the person is entirely clear about what he or she is expected to do. With many things the manager will be able to do this personally, though it is possible with some technical tasks that certain demonstrations might be better done by someone else. Do beware here, however, of assuming that someone who can do something, even who can do it with a degree of excellence, is automatically able to describe to others how he or she does it. This is most often a fallacy, and the technique of sitting down one person with another, more expert, and simply saying, 'Watch', is suspect. Certainly care is needed with what is still sometimes referred to as the 'sit by Nellie' way of training; it can sometimes simply be a way for managers to avoid their responsibilities.

A process of prompting questions to be sure that someone is now clear what is required should accompany the two stages described above. Such questions must not be censorious. If you say something like, 'Right, I'm sure that's clear, any questions?', the danger is that it will put people off asking anything for fear that you will think less well of them if they do. As any confusion can lengthen the whole process unnecessarily, care is needed here.

## 3. Allow practice

At this stage the person must be allowed to have a go, with

you, the manager, watching. All may be well and no further action may be necessary (maybe a written note of some sort by way of reminder?). But the role of the manager is to watch and to assess how things are done, and sometimes a further stage is called for.

## 4. Provide assistance to get it right

Here, if necessary, you may need to provide further assistance. Again care is necessary. An immediate negative response may upset people and put off the moment when they get the hang of something. It is often best to get or encourage the other person to analyse what he or she has done, to prompt him or her to talk it through out loud, as it were. Asking questions such as, 'How did that go?', 'Did you get everything right?', 'How might you have done it differently?', can act to bring out short-falls. Then a second layer of questions may be necessary: 'Why did that happen?', 'How can you make sure it doesn't happen next time?', and so on. It may seem quicker just to say: 'No, do it this way', but it is less effective in prompting learning than is counselling to get the staff member to tease out the solution – one that will then be remembered and used next time.

## 5. Practise again (and again)

Sometimes further practice is necessary. This might mean doing it once more with your supervision, or it might be better to disappear and leave the staff member to practise further quietly on his or her own. You might set a time on this: 'I'll pop back in an hour and see how you're doing.' Or you might leave it with him or her – 'Let me know if you have any more problems', whatever seems appropriate.

# 6. Encourage throughout the process

This is important, and may sometimes mean *finding* an opportunity to praise (and perhaps to continue to explain if the task is something no one gets right instantly). A feeling of making progress can shorten the learning process and thus the time all this takes.

*Note:* in approaching the task reviewed above, remember to keep the perspective of the trainees firmly in mind. What is obvious to you may not be obvious to them. You have to remember their frame of reference. Ask yourself: what experience do they have of this task? If none, can it be equated to something else that they do have experience of and which exhibits similar characteristics? Such questions and their answers can help you position things in an appropriate way. Remember too that if you have to go back to basics this may be only because someone lacks certain experience, so do not make someone feel bad about it.

Similarly you need to bear in mind the habits of the past. Sometimes these can be very strong and difficult to break, even when it is well accepted that they should change. One area where I notice this regularly is in dealing with training in business writing skills. People may want to change, but habits of writing are deeply ingrained and this fact needs to be accommodated when new approaches are mooted.

The boxed section below sets out an example relating to a simple, specific development task, showing how it can be tackled in this kind of way.

## Coaching in action: example

Here we review the principles against a particular task: the interactive communication involved in *handling complaints* as might have to be undertaken by various categories of support staff.

1. *Select an example:* (this might specify the nature of the complaint and the characteristics of the person making it, say on the telephone).
2. *Review background facts:* this might involve looking at policy (money back, no questions asked or whatever) and the information that would need to be to hand to deal effectively with such a complaint (product information, customer order record, etc).
3. *Plan the action necessary:* given the example, planning for contacts which, almost by definition, are unique (and certainly seen as wholly individual by complainants) can be in outline only – but a general view of how such things are handled is nevertheless useful.
4. *Agree the details with the trainees:* if analysis afterwards is going to be useful this is important. Your comments will need to be about what *they* decided and agreed to do, and you do not want them saying something like, 'I never felt it was a good way forward anyway.'
5. *Agree what your role will be:* if training is going to involve observing a real call then whether or not you are available to take over and rescue the situation if necessary needs to be clear. Remember that unplanned intervention will always upset staff, who will doubtless feel that, whatever the difficulty, they were – *just about to get it right.*
6. *Observe:* watch and listen to how something goes. In the example it might be a real telephone call (you might have to ask to be summoned quickly when the right kind of call comes in); or an expected call to allow it all to be observed (eg, making a call to someone who has been promised a call back).

Here observation needs to address the technical nature of the task to ensure that it is being completed appropriately, in this case noting such things as:

■ Did they really listen carefully to what was said?
■ Did they make it clear they were listening?

■ Did they note, accurately, the details referred to during the conversation?

■ Were they suitably sympathetic (while not perhaps accepting blame at this stage)?

■ Did the complaint need clarifying and was that done effectively (an angry outburst can be difficult to follow, for instance)?

■ Was the complaint summarized to double check that both parties were talking about exactly the same thing?

■ What checks were made on the facts (in files, on screen or whatever)?

■ Was any necessary wait while this was done made acceptable or was there an offer to phone back?

■ What action was suggested or answer given to resolve the problem?

■ Was the way of handling the complaint appropriate (to the customer and the organization)?

■ Was any necessary apology sincere and appropriate? (And was it personally put – 'I am sorry' – without the blame being avoided? An apologetic note may be needed throughout.)

■ Was any follow-up action appropriate, made clear and agreed with the customer and noted for future action, with, say, a written apology to be sent promptly?

This kind of informed observation clearly needs some preparation. You need to be aware of what should happen, the sequence in which things should be addressed and have a clear idea of how it should all be done.

7. *Analyse what happened afterwards:* this should be done, as has been said, without leading the trainee too much (see comments made earlier in this chapter) and in light of the plan for observation referred to in 6, above.

8. *Link lessons to follow-up action:* at this point you may need to summarize, to refer to written guidelines, or notes may need

to be made (by either or both parties) relative to action on future occasions.

9. *Arrange and agree follow-up action and timing:* if you feel there is a need to spend more time on the matter, then a follow-up session may be necessary and should be scheduled for a specific date (otherwise good general intentions can easily be overtaken by events). This may need confirming in writing, especially if it is complex. Perhaps several, staged additional sessions are necessary, perhaps a project of some sort for the trainee is to be specified and set to take place between one session and the next.

10. *End on a note of encouragement:* and link to whatever comes next.

Note: the chain of events that must take place must be tailored to the particular circumstances. This is a fairly typical example, but while some things may not need to be so complex, others might need a chain of events that runs through several sessions and across a longer period of time (days or weeks).

# Utilizing appropriate methods

Several training methods, beyond simple advice and counselling, can routinely be built into this sort of coaching. Beyond these, it can be linked to any other methodology, or combination of methodologies, from the training armoury. Some of the main methods are discussed below.

## Demonstration

This is important; there is no substitute for seeing. How it is done and who it is that does it will depend on the skill being developed. One thing should always be borne in mind, however: when it is done it must work. This may imply practice (by the manager), careful choice regarding who else undertakes the demonstration, or careful selection of a case (as with the example of complaint handling used above). In the latter case, indeed with anything where perfection cannot be guaranteed, a range of examples may produce enough things going well to establish credibility and make an effective lesson.

The moral for the manager is to exercise care. If you say something like, 'I will show you how, just watch', then your planning and skills must be up to it. That is not, of course, to say that a manager must be expert in everything. After all, 'You don't have to be able to lay eggs to be a chicken farmer', as the old saying has it. But if you say you can, you better deliver if credibility is to be preserved!

## Role-play

This is investigated as a formal technique later: here suffice to say that it has a role as part of explanation, demonstration and particularly in the analysis that follows. If you are trying to prompt a discussion and get someone to float ideas about ways of doing things then, certainly with interactive skills, this technique works well. Often there is a case in mind already. For example, with the topic of complaint handling referred to, a call is undertaken and observed. That observation shows that there are lessons to be learnt, so role-play might then be used, informally, between you and the trainee. This might only be for a couple of minutes. For instance, you ask how else something could have been done: 'When they said, "I just don't believe you!" what else might you have said? Let me act as the customer, and we'll run the conversation between us for a moment.' Then the conversation is held between you and lessons that it may produce can be discussed further.

Role-play might need more setting up the first time it is done, and it always needs to be clear to both parties just what is under review and how it will be done, but it can also become routine. If you regularly do this with people they will quickly get the message, especially if they perceive it to be useful.

## Checklists and manuals

A variety of forms of written material can be used in this context. This is especially useful when you know the session will repeat (through staff turnover, perhaps) and it is worthwhile writing up something. Again, complaint handling is a good example. It may well be that a fair number of people around the organization need to know how to do this right and material created as part of teaching them to do so will pay for the time it takes.

Such material can be designed with a self-contained quality to it. This might be programmed learning (in text or computer form) that takes trainees through the principles, asks questions and takes them back to reinforce matters where answers are not correct.

Whatever the methodology, on-the-job coaching and training is, for many managers, a prime part of the way in which their development responsibilities are implemented.

# Learning on the job

Another principle worth bearing in mind is that of building learning of some sort into activities that would occur in any case. If this can be done then time is saved almost by definition. This is certainly possible with many executive skills, as one example will illustrate.

In one company with whom I undertook training work on presentational skills, they arranged to reinforce formal courses with practice. This is, after all, a skill where practice is essential (however good an initial course). Certain regular meetings were identified and it was made mandatory that any significant contribution that could be anticipated in advance must, for a period, be made formally. The individual had to stand up and was encouraged to use visual aids. In this way the number of presentations they made was artificially increased, and with it the practice they got. Certain 'presentations' could be further designated for subsequent discussion. Preparation also provided an opportunity to seek counselling. All increased the skill that people developed.

It is worth seeking other such opportunities. Little time or planning is necessary, especially if it is originated, as in this case, at the same time as any more formal training input on the same subject.

# An economy of scale

One thing that you should avoid with all this, if possible, is unnecessary repetition. Keep a watch out for individuals with similar development needs. If James and Julie both need some strengthening in the same way there is sense in getting them together. This may not only save you time, it may be more fun and interesting for them and more motivational too, each knowing they are not the only one having difficulty with a particular thing.

A further economy of scale comes with matters of reinforcement (or matters new to all) when action can be directed towards improvement at group meetings. In most organizations teams do get together and meet on a regular basis. Such meetings may be for various reasons, for example to:

■ disseminate or exchange information;
■ discuss matters, contribute to or make decisions;
■ motivate people;

■ check progress towards targets and take action to fine-tune results;
■ spark creativity (as in a brainstorming session).

There can usefully be a development element to the agenda of staff meetings of this sort. When there is it does not necessarily need to be labelled 'training', but it does need to be organized. A manager can use a session at a group meeting for a variety of purposes such as to:

■ improve the basis of knowledge (of products or procedures, for example);
■ introduce new areas of skill not required in the past;
■ reinforce existing skills or refine them in the light of change;
■ practise a technique or skill.

In addition to just achieving whatever is required, such sessions are an opportunity to get people involved and participating, and thinking. Some topics may need to be revisited regularly just to give existing, but important, skills an additional honing. If this can be done in a way that adds variety – and avoids the group feeling, 'Oh, no, not that again' – so much the better.

A good way of doing this is to use individuals to hook into a topic again in a new or topical way. The opportunity for this may be spotted in one-to-one sessions with individuals. You touch on a topic, their thinking or experience is good, and you can set something up for a planned meeting – 'That's interesting. Can you think it through a little more and prepare to speak about how you reckon this problem can be solved when the group meets next week? It ought to lead into some useful discussion.' This gives you a way of putting ideas over to the group that are not labelled as, 'The manager says do it this way.' You need to give someone due warning and an opportunity to prepare in doing this (if you unleash it on them *at* a meeting it may well be resented and the session may go less well). Your team will quickly get used to the fact that you do this, individuals may well be flattered to be asked to do such things too, so it may be important to share round the lead in such little projects progressively.

Other useful ways of revisiting topics with the group include the use of training films; this is dealt with on page 66. Also the use of exercises; you may be able to create such things yourself, linked very specifically to current operational matters. Alternatively, a great deal of ready-made material can be bought in to act as the foundation of such group activities.

The possibilities here are wide ranging. Exercises and the like can be made a regular, expected and valued feature of such meetings. All that is necessary is some thought beforehand and the time spent can then produce a developmental boost for a whole team of people.

A further technique is relevant here: coaching that is done by someone other than you.

# Mentoring

One approach: low cost, practical and useful – and often fun – that can keep people updated and able to perform well whatever is demanded of you, and actively assist career development, is that of mentoring.

## What is a mentor?

A mentor is someone who exercises a low key and informal developmental coaching role – one of positive, practical value – and who enjoys the satisfaction of helping people develop and seeing them excel. They must willingly commit time to the process, but such time need not be great. Even so, finding that time may be challenging. It can help to organize mentoring on a swap basis: a colleague will make a regular input to one of your team and you do the same for one of their people. The key thing is that anyone acting as a mentor must be willing to spend such time *regularly*. Some real continuity is clearly essential. A mentor is rarely someone's line manager; rather it is someone *other than* the direct boss. He or she may be from elsewhere in the organization – or indeed from outside it.

Usually, if such relationships last, they start as one-way – they help the person being mentored – but as time passes, they may well become more two-way; indeed perhaps the person on the mentor side rather expects this. There is no reason why someone cannot have regular contact with several mentors, with each different relationship achieving different things.

An effective mentor can be a powerful force for development. So how do you find one? In some organizations this process is centralized and formalized: people are allocated or can request one, making this a regular development technique. Equally you may need to prompt matters, suggesting it to a more senior manager, or direct to a potential candidate. What starts as an apparently one-off arrangement may act as a catalyst, and lead on to something more substantial.

## What makes it work?

Mentors must have authority, be capable and confident, and thus are likely to be reasonably senior. They need suitable knowledge, experience and expertise, plus good counselling skills, and a degree of clout.

Mentoring demands a series of meetings, these creating a thread of review, discussion and activity within the continuity of operations. These meetings may be informal, but most do need an agenda. More important, they need to be constructive. If they are, then one thing will naturally lead to another – a variety of occasions can be utilized to maintain the dialogue. A meeting; followed by a brief encounter, say over a drink; a project and a promise to spend a moment on feedback; a few e-mails passing in different directions – all may contribute. All such activity runs in parallel with any more formal development that this or other procedures initiate. What makes this process useful is the commitment and quality of the mentor. Where such relationships can be set up, and work well, they add a powerful dimension to the ongoing development cycle, one that it is difficult to imagine being bettered in any other way. The regularity and ready access involved is somewhat akin to being able to speak to a schoolteacher outside of class in a way that takes matters forward.

Topics chosen may be general – a series of things all geared, let's say, to improving presentations skills, and thus ranging from help with preparation to a critique of a rehearsal. Or they may focus very specifically, aiming to ensure that an individual report is well written and well received, for example.

The power of mentoring to prompt change is considerable. Personally, early in my career, as my job began to demand that I wrote reports and proposals and then articles, I had to accept that this was not my greatest strength. One more senior colleague was, however, a great mentor. His influence was twofold. First he offered practical advice, critiquing my writing and encouraging me to actively learn more about how to improve it (principally by reading and attending short courses). As I understood more about how to do it and the effect I was striving to achieve, became more conscious of the process and listened to his advice, my style improved. But secondly, and just as important, his role encouraged and motivated: he convinced me I could write better, and made me delight in finding a good form of words and expressing a message with appropriate precision so that I was likely to achieve my purpose. Even so, faced with writing my first management book, left alone I would probably have passed – 'It's not my thing.' But he cajoled me into tackling it. His input not only improved my writing but also led to a situation where, for many years now, articles and books have been a significant and ongoing part of my work portfolio. So much so that now, with more than 50 business titles published, I have had something completely different published: a book of light-hearted travel writing (*First Class at Last!* from Marshall Cavendish). This is a direct, dramatic and long-term outcome of good mentoring.

Either party, of course, can originate the topics or skills that mentoring addresses. The mentor can indicate where specific help is necessary, or the individual can recognize and request it. Thus mentoring encounters can:

▦   be planned and long term;
▦   link to other activity (both operational and developmental);
▦   be opportunistic, scheduled at short notice to tie in with events;
▦   consist of one exchange or a number of linked ones;
▦   add positively or warn of dangers ahead.

Yet, individual sessions may be brief, and their motivational impact as important as the instruction they provide. Overall, continuity must be maintained, avoiding long gaps and with time scheduled for mutual convenience. Keeping a log of mentoring sessions is useful, either because they are or will be linked to formal systems (such as job appraisal) or just to help prove its practical worth. Mentoring can work in parallel to coaching by a line manager; together the two things are very powerful.

Even so, sometimes there is a need to deliver a development message that is substantial and which must involve a number of people. Then more formal training is necessary. This too is something you can undertake, as we see in the next two chapters.

# 5

# Formal training: deciding content and method

*Whatever is worth doing at all is worth doing well.*

*The Earl of Chesterfield*

There is an old story of the manager who pledged to find a one-armed management trainer. He was asked why. 'Just to have someone who doesn't say, "On the one hand this ... and on the other hand that ...",' he replied. So: consider putting over a training message. On the one hand, training presentations should be straightforward. After all, they are for the most part factually based. There is a body of material to put across and, if you know your topic, you should be on strong ground. Further, as has been said, for the most part people like receiving training. The culture of any good organization will encourage it, and see that it becomes associated with progress, greater personal interest and improvement. Indeed, ensuring that this is so may well be part of your job.

But – there is so often a but – on the other hand there can be difficulties. It is not like chatting to someone over your desk. There are expectations, there are risks, and you are, inevitably to a certain extent, exposed. There are, however, ways in which to build on the expectations and to tackle the risks in a manner that will create a satisfactory whole. This chapter sets out to review both.

Preparation is the key to successful presentation. Do not doubt it, underestimate it, or skimp it; you will do so at your peril. A good speaker can range far and wide from their plan, but (with rare exception) they will have thought about it and, while the degree of preparation will of course vary, that it should always take place is a fundamental rule.

# Preparation – first steps

Assuming you already have a clear programme outline, we concentrate here on preparing the presentational elements of a session. This starts with consideration of the group, and the individual members of it. In training the numbers are normally manageable, with perhaps 8 to 20 people being best, with a few more on some occasions. This may not be as daunting as a massed group of, say, 400 in a conference centre, though you may sometimes have to cope with large numbers, at anything from departmental meetings or sales conferences to gatherings of the whole company. In any case, every size of group presents a different challenge. Whoever they are, and however many of them there are, you need to think about how people will feel about the training.

It helps to have clear answers to a number of questions as preparation is started:

▓ Who are those in the group?
▓ Do you know them?
▓ Do they know each other?
▓ How long have they been with the organization?
▓ What job function and level of seniority do they have?

- What previous training have they had?
- What will be their expectations of, and attitude to, the training? (It may also be useful to ask the same of their manager/s if that is not you.)

Such considerations may consist of anything from simply a few moments' thought, to some checking, or the circulation of some kind of pre-course questionnaire. You can't ever know too much about the group. Besides, it avoids surprises, some of which may result in a need to adjust the plan so that you are able to cope with them (a fact that will be vouched for by many). Those who have been faced with an all-woman group, for example, after planning for a mixed-sex group – or as once happened to me, a group where half the participants could not speak English – will confirm the need for adjustment to the training plan. The most bizarre case I have ever heard of was a presenter who, having prepared his input around a veritable surfeit of slides, realized – belatedly – that 80 per cent of the group in question were blind!

Before turning to the detail of what preparation entails, it is appropriate to mention one very important factor: your *lecturing notes*. This may seem like running ahead, but as preparation leads up to the point where, with the right kind of aide-mémoire in front of you, you start the session, it will make better sense to consider your lecturing notes as we proceed.

While the detail any individual will need will vary, practically everyone needs some notes. Anyone new to training should probably not attempt to work without some clear notes to guide them. But what exactly is appropriate? One aspect that needs to be worked out is the style of notes that suits you. It can be in any style you like, but it must be practical. For instance:

- A loose-leaf ring binder may be best, ensuring that material stays open and flat in front of you (a binder with pockets in the front and/or rear covers allows you to store 'exhibits' that go with the course material – a brochure perhaps – conveniently in the same binder).

■ A4 pages may be better than cards (which some like, and which may suit working from a lectern) as you can see a reasonable amount of what is ahead at any one time. This also allows paper copies of slides to be put in the same binder.

■ Writing/typing on one side of the paper allows additional material to be added, or amendments made easily.

■ Use a suitable size of words, or type. This affects how you use the notes. I find, as a spectacles wearer, that when standing I can read normal typed material best from a binder placed on top of a hard briefcase (or something of similar size) laid flat on a table, rather than on the table itself.

■ If using an A4 page, a good bold, coloured line dividing it into two or three segments, or enclosing a section in a box, will give the eye several smaller areas on which to progressively focus, and make it easier to keep track of how far you have gone as you proceed.

■ Always number the pages; there may well be quite a lot of material. Some people like to number in reverse order, say with page 40 at the front and page 1 at the end. This helps to estimate the time remaining (you may well come to be able to estimate how long a typical page of your style of guiding notes takes you to work through), and still acts to keep things in order.

Such notes are *not* in any sense a script. Reading material verbatim has little or no place in training. There are some short exceptions, like a definition or technicality that may need to be quoted precisely. Reading risks not only sounding dull, but it can be difficult to do (try reading something without stumbling). Extemporizing from good notes is easier, and will produce a better effect. While everyone needs to find – by experiment no doubt – what suits them, an example may serve as a model and prompt thinking. Simple symbols or initials can be used to save space, and act as a more obvious prompt than simply a word:

S        indicates when to show a slide (S1, S2, etc).

Ex      indicates when there is to be *delegate* participation (and can expand on how, as in 'working in pairs': Ex (x2).

?        specific *questions* to be asked of the group.

Eg      *examples* of what is being discussed.

OP      used as a prefix to the others when there is something *optional* (having material that can easily be added or not helps you keep to time).

You may want to evolve others for a variety of points:

■ summarize on flipchart;
■ hand out materials;
■ introduce/show film/video;
■ tell anecdote, and so on.

Good bold prompts like this are invaluable and you will come to recognize them instantly.

Now, it is not suggested, at least not to begin with, that preparation starts with a blank sheet of paper and ends with a complete documented session in one simple step. So how does one go about it? How do you produce good training, yet not take forever? It needs a logical process, and several aspects are involved.

# Materials

Here decisions are made about what materials will be used, by whom, why, and to what effect. Actually preparing them, making slides or writing notes, comes later. Fashions change in this area (and attitudes vary in different organizations and in different countries). Some favour extensive materials, some minimal notes; different topics will also need different back up. What materials are necessary 'on the day' should certainly be considered: papers, exhibits to be in front of the group during the session; and what résumé material is necessary to form a source of reference after the course.

The former includes a variety of items, from a group that is too complex to make into a slide but which everyone must look at together, to an exercise sheet with only a handful of words on it, but which is to be completed during the session. With résumé notes, the current feeling (at least in the UK) seems to have swung towards something shorter rather than longer, though whether this is because a book-style résumé is unnecessary, unused or simply expensive and time-consuming to produce, is a mute point. Certainly the repetition of a résumé aids learning.

## The format of the speaker's notes

To give an example of the sort of notes you may have in front of you during your presentation, let's use a presentations skills course as an example. What follows is by way of an illustration. It is not suggested that this is the only, or necessarily the best way in which to begin such a session (though in the right circumstances, notes along these lines work well); nor is it suggested that the format of notes shown should be followed slavishly. However, it does allow the principles involved to be illustrated. Ultimately, what matters is that the individual finds a comfortable and practical format with which to work.

First, a possible introductory section to such a course is set out verbatim (though it is difficult to describe the full effect of a presentation in print); see Example 1. Then the speaker's notes from which this might have been presented are shown in Example 2. In real life this is best done in (at least) two colours. To complete the picture, imagine a first introductory slide being shown during these brief few moments (something to tie in with something said). Then Example 3 shows how some of the factors included in the introduction to illustrate presentation in action can be used to prompt an early discussion designed to get everyone in a group involved and open up the topic and highlight key issues. Together these exhibits illustrate an encapsulation of training in action.

So, now we turn to the sequence referred to above, and start with the verbatim text of the introductory minutes of a presentation skills session.

# Example 1: What was actually said

(People have assembled for the session. Informal discussion has no doubt been taking place, and we join the session as the clock hits 9 am and the trainer makes a formal start.)

Right. Let's make a start. Thank you all for being in good time – we have a busy day ahead. As you know, the topic is 'Making effective presentations', and the session is predominantly participative.

Briefly, first we'll run over a few administrative points, then I shall set the scene and we'll discuss how I've done that to begin to highlight some of the issues. At that stage too, as not everyone knows each other, we'll go round the room and give everyone the opportunity to introduce themselves, though as I've said I have to make the first presentation of the day!

So, admin first (here the trainer runs over a few points, ranging perhaps from when notes will be distributed to where the conveniences are located).

Now to the topic of the day. You all make presentations, and do so for a variety of different reasons. There is a common factor here that affects everyone. This can be illustrated by communications you receive having made a presentation – maybe a letter from a customer or an internal memo from a director. There are some which, though they start ever so politely, 'We were grateful for your presentation', then continue with a firm 'but'. And the net result is no order; no agreement; no go-ahead for the plans you presented, or whatever.

We all know the feeling. And after all we had done! But why? Afterwards we start asking questions about what happened, about the presentation:

- Was it too long, or too short?
- Did they not understand it, particularly if it was technical?
- Did you inadvertently pick your nose, or holes in a member of the group?

At this stage you will never know for certain, but sometimes we know there were problems and we begin to say, 'If only ... I shouldn't have' to ourselves. We do know it could have been better and, worse, we often feel that if it had been a simple one-to-one meeting rather than a presentation, it would certainly have been better.

You may know the old saying: 'The human brain is a wonderful thing – it starts working on the day you are born – goes on and on, and only stops on the day you have to speak in public.'

Often, making what we did better only needed some more preparation beforehand. Occasionally what went wrong is less clear, or there may be more serious omissions. Afterwards it is certainly too late ... there is usually no second chance ... and no second prize.

Today, we shall do two things – review the process of presentation, and practise it. To be specific, we'll review the structure of a presentation, and the techniques that make it possible to prepare and deliver an effective one.

And practice ... that's you on TV. Sounds a bit traumatic – by the end of the day you'll hate yourself, your colleagues, and especially me! Not really. Actually, while it does give you an opportunity to see how you perform, it is also important in providing real-life examples of the sort of things that crop up for us to all discuss. I'm sure you will find it useful. More of this later. I'll make quite clear how it will all work before we get to that stage. The emphasis on both the review and the practice is deliberate. It is designed to help:

■ make presenting easier;
■ make it more certain and, above all, more effective;
■ even to make it more fun.

Now, are there any questions at this point before we move on?

# Example 2 – Speaker's notes

## Making effective presentations

Intro:
– admin         Time/participation
                Timing
                Notes
                Questions (link to training plan)
                Breaks/lunch
                Messages
Set the scene   The topic of the day – presentations
                      Different reasons/common importance
                      Common factor – a lot hanging on
                      them
                      Internal memo → no agreement to plans

                Inquest: despite effort — what happened?
                      ? long/short
                      ? technical
                      + holes/nose

                Not 100% ... but 'if only...'

                'The human brain is a wonderful thing – it starts
                working the day you are born – goes on and

on, and only stops on the day you have to speak in public.'
Improvement – more preparation
minor/major problems

Afterwards too late – no second chance/prize

Today:  review the structure/techniques process:
and practice – TV
'real-life examples'
discussion
– no problem
(details to come)

Emphasis:
    – make it easier
    – certain/effective
    – fun

(questions)

→      discussion
      (see checklist)

– what went on (and did not) over the last few minutes?
    Example?

After the pause at the end of the introductory session there may be questions from the group. Once these have been dealt with appropriately, the trainer can again take the initiative.

A discussion at this point can be made to involve everybody, will air the issues that will be dealt with further during the day, will put people more at ease (video work is somewhat worrying), and will begin to ease people into the topic.

# Example 3: Prompting discussion

Such an initial discussion can be started with a question: 'Think about what I have just done in that introductory few moments; can we list any techniques that were involved – and indeed, any that were not, and perhaps should have been?' Then points can be listed – perhaps taking every member of the group in turn – (and perhaps a few words said about each). These might include:

- Giving a clear brief (was it?).
- An early link to the specific jobs of those in the group.
- An early, rhetorical, question (why?).
- Use of a quote.
- A little humour.
- A dramatic pause.
- Putting people at ease, or at least starting to, about the video.
- A lead into a discussion and participation.
- An opportunity to ask questions.
- Use of visual aid(s).

Similarly, what was *not* done or used? For example: no handout (yet), no one addressed by name, and so on.

Again, this is not the only way of proceeding, but it helps complete a comprehensive example of this part of the proceedings. For instance, humour is not always necessary, and certainly you must not overdo it. In the example above the quotation brings a smile and is a safe way of adding a lighter touch; after all one of the jobs of the introduction is to put people at their ease. Take care, however. If you actually say something like, 'This will amuse you ...', then it better do so.

Any training session is an event. It is an experience for those who attend (and for the trainer for that matter). What participants take away is an amalgam of everything that has happened. It blends elements including what they heard, saw and did, and can involve other senses. What did they touch – in an equipment demonstration, perhaps? They take away impressions, some of which will last; others need, and may receive, progressive reinforcements; some will, inevitably, be rapidly forgotten. (See the next chapter for more on how people learn and retain information.)

Participants also take away, or experience, or use, materials. There are a variety of these, and they fall into a number of distinct categories. Some such are for the trainer, some for the participants, and some for both. Let us take those for the trainer first.

# The materials you, the trainer, need

Perhaps the most important items are the 'lecture notes' – the guiding documentation the trainer plans to have in front of him or her during the session to act as a kind of 'route map'. These set out the structure, content and method. Whatever they look like – the only real criterion is that they suit *you*.

Secondly, the trainer needs a set of those materials the participants will have issued to them. Thirdly, a number of other things may be needed, for example:

- equipment;
- exhibits;
- the 'trainer's guide' for a (rented) video;
- visual aids;
- props.

Some of these are commented upon below.

# Visual aids

Visual aids are very important. Remember that one of the factors mentioned earlier was the power of a visual image rather than an aural image.

The first category is those aids that are used to add a simple message to the proceedings. These have two different advantages. *For the trainer* they can act as an additional progressive guide to the structure and content of the session, as with the way one would work through a list of slides. *Note:* visual aids are a *support* to the session. The tail should not wag the dog, they are there to reinforce, exemplify and illustrate what is being presented or discussed, rather than lead it. They must not take over. A presentation that has no slides may be dull in comparison with one that does. On the other hand, one that uses too many, particularly checklist-style slides (ie, predominantly words), may become over-structured around their use in a way that is also dull or becomes too predictable.

*For the group* they represent a proven aid to learning and, no less important, some variety. In addition, they may provide other effects, including humour (for example, cartoons work well in training provided they are relevant).

In summary, visual aids can:

▓ Present a great deal of information quickly.
▓ Improve the understanding of a presentation.
▓ Give visible structure to the verbal communication.
▓ Allow a visualization of the main thrust of an argument, and 'position' the message before it is examined in detail.

The most common forms of visual aid are:

▓ flipcharts;
▓ slides;
▓ table-top presenters;
▓ fixed whiteboards;
▓ handouts.

# General principles of preparing visual aids

▓ Keep the content simple. *Note:* the advent of Microsoft's invaluable PowerPoint has resulted in the phrase 'death by PowerPoint'. There is a tendency to use too many slides; especially to be avoided is putting too much text on a slide and – worst of all – reading it all out slavishly.

▓ Restrict the number of words:
- use single words to give structure, headings, or short statements;
- do not cause the aid to look cluttered and complicated;
- personalize the firm's name or logo (or course title) where possible.

▓ Use diagrams, graphs, etc where possible to present figures. Never read figures alone without visual support.

▓ Build in variety within the overall common theme:
- use colour;
- build in variations of the forms of aids used.

▓ Emphasize the theme and the structure:
- continually use one of the aids as a recurring reminder of the objective and agenda (eg, prepared flipchart);
- make logical use of the aids (eg, slides as a base for presentation; flipchart or whiteboard for highlighting comment).

▓ Ensure the content of the visual matches what you say – make the content relevant.

▓ Ensure the visuals can be seen:
- Are they clear? (Never ask, 'Can you see that?' You should *know* it is legible.)
- What are the room limitations?
- What are the equipment limitations?
- Use strong colour.
- Beware of normal typeface reproduced on slides unless enlarged.
- Ensure the layout emphasizes the meaning the aid should convey.

> *Note:* Those wanting to avoid the hazards of slides with a surfeit of text might check the book *Killer Presentations* (Nick Oulton, How to Books), which provides inspiration and an antidote.

Finally, in what is an important area, the main rules in using visual aids are:

■ Talk to the group, not the visuals.
■ Use colour to highlight key points.
■ Talk to the group while writing on a visual aid.
■ Avoid impeding the group's view of visual aids.
■ Explain graphs and figures or any complex chart.
■ Remove an aid immediately when it is no longer required (with PowerPoint the most important key on the computer is B – it blanks the screen, and returns it back to where you were when you want to move on).
■ Tell the participants what they will receive as copies. It is often useful to issue slides in hard copy after the session.

## Equipment and exhibits

I once worked with a US consultant who ran an excellent seminar on pricing strategy. If such a seminar was done in a hotel meeting room he always ordered two hard-boiled eggs with his breakfast, one brown, another white, along with a raw onion. He received some funny looks, but used both as exhibits, props if you prefer; the first to illustrate customers' fickle attitude to price (people will pay more for brown eggs than white), and the onion to make a point about market segments. So, as this clearly illustrates, the materials a trainer might need at a session are many and various.

It is an area for which you may usefully evolve a personal checklist. Some of the items on this will be straightforward. For instance, you may list equipment you use regularly, and having mentioned equipment, an obvious but often overlooked point is worth stressing: *always, always check all the equipment before the session begins;* not only before, but far enough ahead to have time to rectify any problem. Even small things – a flipchart pen that won't write – causes a momentary hiatus and reflects on your professionalism.

# Using training films

There are numerous producers of training films and much of what they produce is extremely professional, extremely useful and favoured by many.

Too often the film, most often, of course, in DVD form these days, is regarded as an entity in its own right. A good film may well teach lessons of itself, but films are nearly always more powerful as an integrated part of a session or course. If their use is planned in this way you will achieve more from them. But we are running ahead of ourselves. The first job – often by no means straightforward – is to select a film to use.

Film quality does vary. Some films have a well-defined purpose, and will not suit any and every group. The first source of films is the catalogues, though it's worth saying immediately that no trainer should ever use a film that he or she has not viewed in its entirety before the session. The questions the trainer should ask come back to having clear objectives for the session:

- What is the main point that needs to be made to the group?
- Is a film an appropriate way of doing it (or part of it)?
- What attitude changes are involved in the process? Would a film help with this?
- Is the style of the film (the settings and situation) compatible with our organization? If not, can inferences still be drawn from it?

In part, the decision will be influenced by how the film will be used. Will it, for instance, be a curtain raiser, or something to spark discussion, lead into role-play or summarize? How will the film fulfil this role? Some thought here is always sensible; it is rather too common to find a film being included just because 'there should be a film'.

There is certainly more to showing a film than simply saying, 'Now we will look at a film' and pressing the switch. Tina Tietjen, who knows a thing or two about training films and was involved in the early days of Video Arts, set out in a Gower handbook which I edited, an approach to using films which is worth paraphrasing here:

Assuming a film is to be used as part of a fuller training session, the film presenter should do certain preparatory work:

■ View the film completely.
■ Make notes on the following:
  – Significant scenes, which relate to his training message and his organization.
  – Significant phrases and expressions used by the characters, which typify employees in his organization.
  – Any training points picked out captioned in the film.
  – Any 'below the line' training points in the film. These will be points not captioned or mentioned in the dialogue but dropped in for the sharp-eyed trainer to notice. Memorable examples have been the clock in the interviewer's eye line in the Video Arts' selection interviewing film 'Man Hunt', and the incorrect placing of telephones on the desk during the John Cleese scenes in the Video Arts film 'Will You Answer True?'
  – A series of prompts: 'What happened when the customer said, 'They're too expensive'? or, 'What happened when Sheila said she wouldn't cooperate with the new procedures?'
  – Names of the characters, their job titles and relative status.

- Points where the film can be stopped to allow for discussion or role-plays to take place.
■ Read the accompanying discussion leader's guide for ideas on how to use the film.
■ Read any other booklets supplied with the film. Such booklets usually extend the lessons in the film and cover related subjects, which may have not been able to be addressed in the film.
■ See the film through again.
■ Having completed this basic preparation the trainer is in a position to plan the training session and decide the role the film will play within the wider programme.

All of this, like so much that makes training work, is in the area of preparation. Beyond this, the use will be influenced by the nature of the particular film. There are two main types.

# 1. Case study films

These enact a drama, often one involving a series of mistakes, and they typically end with either a series of flashbacks highlighting what went wrong and hence the learning points made, a final scene in which the right way forward is spelt out by one of the characters, or a combination of the two.

Such films make good openers (one classic example many know is the training film 'Who Killed the Sale?'). They allow the scene to be set quickly, and thus the subject broached quickly. In addition, they can highlight likely mistakes, problems or difficult areas without the necessity for examples from within the organization being quoted, and the subsequent awkwardness this can sometimes create. They provide a common framework for discussion, and often lend themselves to re-showing, clip-by-clip, so that more detailed discussion can be prompted.

Such a film may well be best shown in two parts. Stopping it before the final scene explains everything prompts discussion, with the last section being run later. This allows key questions to be posed:

- How did the situation come about?
- Who was at fault?
- How could it have been prevented?
- What are the lessons for the future?

And so on, depending on the topic.

## 2. Right way/wrong way films

These usually start with the wrong way and divide the topic into a number of segments. This type of film may again lend itself to being viewed section by section – with participants discussing what went wrong and why, and reviewing possible better approaches before going on to view the next section. On occasions there is no reason why showing a film should not be spread out over a long period, with the gaps in viewing involving exercises and even role-playing. The film can always be shown a second time later on to give the satisfaction of continuous viewing.

Similar approaches can, of course, be applied to the 'right way' section, with discussion reviewing lessons and, perhaps, action and systems change that should result. Even the right way may be bettered in some organizations; it is the approach that is most important, not a slavish following of some, after all, fictitious procedure.

Films provide a different set of memories, different that is from what is said, discussed or dealt with in other ways. Humour has become a popular way of creating memorable images. Some of the Video Arts' films are now more often called the 'John Cleese films' as a result, though the comedy actor appeared only in a few early titles. Extreme humour runs the danger of obscuring the message, but different producers favour different degrees and styles of humour; as do users and course delegates. If you use films regularly, it may be worth planning the use of different styles from different producers to ensure they continue to add freshness to the sessions in which they are used, and so that people do not come to expect a similar, 'statutory' film every half day or so. As someone once remarked about a particular trainer, 'You can always predict his session, there is one film for every three yards of training.'

That said, showing films can undeniably be useful. They vary the pace, add another element, create additional memories, and can be used to lead into constructive discussion, exercises and role-play of all kinds. As long as they are seen as a support to the session, with a specific part to play, rather than as an end in themselves or an opportunity for the trainer to have a rest, they can contribute – and contribute powerfully. Make them accelerate learning and they can be a regular part of the training you do, an element participants look forward to, and from which they benefit.

If delegates find that a film is not a 'soft option', but leads into a part of the session that is hard work, then the film is being used wisely.

# Participant material

Participants cannot simply sit and listen. They need to participate (we come to the detail of this in Chapter 7), and they need to remember. The materials issued to participants serve both purposes. There is a role for résumé notes, something to remind them of the course content later; and a need for working papers, items the group needs in front of them during the session, to complete exercises and make notes.

Participants' notes are for the participants. An obvious statement, but there can be problems with documents that are designed to be both the résumé notes and the main reference for the trainer. There is no reason why the two should be similar. It is also worth noting at the outset that:

■ Notes can be distributed before, at the start of, during or after a session (or some of each, progressively filling a loose-leaf binder). Remember, people have an irresistible urge to read ahead, so material distributed in advance should not be virtually a verbatim equivalent of what you plan to say and should obviously not include answers to exercises or questions that you plan to pose.

■ Résumé notes need not, in any case, follow what you say slavishly. It may be better to approach topics in another way (in part this creates learning by repetition).

■ Hard copies of slides may form a useful part of the participants' notes.

■ People best remember things they have heard, seen and noted, so notes designed to be annotated where appropriate work well.

■ The total 'pack' that is finally retained should be of reasonable quality (so participants want to keep it), practical (eg, loose-leaf and able to lie flat), and personalized. The latter is important. If the material finally contains an individual participant's notes, indication of emphasis, action points and so on, it will be more likely to be both retained and used.

■ Time and cost are involved. A mammoth book-style handout will take longer, and therefore cost more, to produce (and to print). A compromise between factors is often necessary here.

■ In addition, what is best is also a function of style and fashion. Some organizations favour more or less material; more to be comprehensive, less to make it manageable (some will measure an external training consultant's value by the weight of the handouts they supply, not, it must be said, an infallible guide).

▓ Again, as with so much training, a typical handout 'pack' does not constitute a recommendation for everything, but many events work well with:
   – some pre-course reading (this may be background and might not even be originated by the trainer, eg, an article);
   – some material, predominantly exercises and key points, distributed early in the session;
   – résumé notes, to act as a permanent reference, distributed at the end.

The next question relates to format. What should the handouts look like? How should they be designed? So much more is possible with modern word-processing (and desktop publishing), and the handouts will be valued far more if they look professional. More important is how they work.

The permutations are almost endless, and you need to decide what is right for you. You may want a 'house-style'; alternatively, different topics and sessions may necessitate a different approach. It is horses for courses and up to you.

So all this is worth some time and care; a number of points will assist in ensuring it is right. Participants' notes must:

▓ Be attractive – well produced material (and this need not be elaborately or expensively done) gets more attention paid to it.

▓ Be relevant – and explain why they are. In other words, they need constantly to link to the job in hand, improvements to be made, and so on.

▓ Relate to prior knowledge – taking people forward in comfortable steps from where they are at present.

▓ Present information in 'chunks' – in other words, there should be no sections relying on page upon page of solid text; they need to be structured, with divisions, headings; anything to split it down into bite-sized segments.

▓ Be logical – a step-by-step approach works best, adding details progressively.

- Be memorable – reflecting and linking to the session and the way in which it was presented, and real-life examples and real-life cases help here.
- Aim to change behaviour – with a little repetition, prompting with questions and so on actively assisting learning.
- Contain *options*, digressions adding to the material of the session, with an exercise or project, perhaps.

Also, of course, any material should meet certain practical criteria. It should:

- Be logical – obvious, but sometimes items such as representations of slides can present difficulties.
- Lie flat – using ring binders seems best (which also allows material to be added in future).
- Have space – sufficient for notes, annotations and examples to be added without making the whole effect messy.
- Be 'findable' – consider a table of contents, dividers, numbered pages, colour-codes (or paper), a glossary, further reading list, etc.
- Be illustrated – where explanation can never be sufficient on its own, slides being reproduced, diagrams, flow charts, even pictures can add considerably to its usefulness.
- Finally, the wording – the language – should be appropriate. So some dos and don'ts may be useful and appear in the box below.

## Notes – write right

- Be precise, specific, and make sure that where language is aimed at clear explanation it provides just that (eg, beware of phrases such as '24/7 service' – what exactly does it mean, or words like 'soon' – how soon is soon?).

- Use the active voice; in other words, say 'Use the active voice' not, 'The active voice should be used.'
- Be conversational. Use the word 'you'; people are more likely to learn if it is phrased for them.
- Be positive rather than negative (ie, many don'ts are better stated as dos).
- Explain reasons. Do not say 'You should ask questions', say 'If you ask the right questions, in the right way, the information you obtain will make it easier to ...'.
- Use any humour carefully.
- Avoid stereotypes: if possible every person in stories, cases and examples should not be men (or women). Be careful of age and minority groups – though one has to be realistic, and descriptive. For instance, 'chairperson' is clear and well used, while 'salesperson' does not have as specific a meaning as 'salesman' (one meaning anyone involved in selling in whatever way, the other usually meaning the field salesperson, or representative).
- Watch out for over-used stock phrases and, of course, avoid clichés like the plague (sic).
- Do explain abbreviations, at least the first time.
- Do check exact meanings. In multinational organizations especially, simple matters can cause confusion (eg, if we 'table something at a meeting', in the United States this means we will not discuss it; in the UK it means that we will).
- If, like me, you must watch your spelling, use a spell-check program (remember that it won't check/cheque everything), or ask someone suitable to look through the material and correct it.

There is another item amongst the material (documentation might be a better word in this case) and that is the notification that must go to participants before the session. This is an area that can suffer from lack of thought. As one who has arrived at client companies to conduct a programme and found myself facing a group of people whose briefing has consisted of a little more than: 'Be there at 9 am', I know it is important.

The thought required and the time it takes are not prohibitive, and a session is likely to go very much better if people not only know what it is about and why they are there, but are committed to its success. The checklist below shows how this can be simply, yet comprehensively, done.

---

## Checklist: Pre-course notification

Make sure a note goes to every participant announcing the training event and briefing them as to its nature. (*Note:* remember that the note may instruct, suggest or attempt to persuade people to attend. It may go from the trainer or a line manager, or both – there is good sense in 'the boss' being seen to be involved.)

In every case, make sure that it states:

■ what the topic is;
■ why it is being scheduled (and why now);
■ what specific objectives are set;
■ what benefit they will receive from it (personally) in their jobs, perhaps as specifically as what they will be able to do after attending that they could not do, or could not do so well, before;
■ what participation will be expected;
■ any preparation that is necessary (and follow-up that must be fitted in);
■ anything they should bring (from the obvious, something to write with, to the less obvious, a calculator, diary, files, literature, projects, etc);
■ who else is attending;
■ who is conducting the session;

▓ any administrative and organizational points:
  – When it is.
  – Where it is (and how to find your way there, if necessary).
  – Timings.
  – How messages will be handled.
  – How participants should dress. (For our chosen example, where they will be making a presentation, formal 'office wear' is no doubt appropriate; on some sessions an opportunity to be less formal than usual can be taken.)
  – 'House rules' (eg, is there somewhere for smokers to go?).
  – Expenses (if relevant).
  – Meal requests (vegetarians?).
  – An acknowledgement (or even a thank you) if arrangements cut into private time – perhaps they have to travel to the training centre or venue on a Sunday night to start early on Monday morning.

As well as the kind of information mentioned above, further notes can be given to delegates as part of documentation on the day. The box below is an example of the kind of thing that I mean. Feel free to adapt it or use it as the basis for a document suitable for your own organization.

## Notes for delegates

(An example of a document issued to delegates at the start of a course or ahead of attendance.)

This manual contains all the basic details of this training programme. Further papers will be distributed progressively during the course so that a complete record will be available by the last session.

This is *your* seminar, and represents a chance to say what you think – so please do say it. Everyone can learn from the comments of others and the discussion they prompt.

Exchange of experience is as valuable as the formal lectures –

but you need to *listen carefully* and try to understand other points of view if this is to work.

Do support your views with facts in discussion; use examples and stick to the point.

Keep questions and comments succinct – do not monopolize the proceedings, but let others have a say so that various viewpoints can be discussed.

Make points in context as they arise. Remember that participation is an attitude of mind. It includes listening as well as speaking, but also certainly includes constructive disagreement where appropriate.

Make notes as the meeting progresses. There is notepaper provided in this binder. Formal notes will provide an aide-mémoire of the content and coverage, so any additional notes should primarily link to your job and to action on your return to work. Even a few action points noted per session can act as a catalyst and help ensure action follows attendance.

A meeting with colleagues, staff or your manager on your return to normal working can be valuable; it acts as a bridge between ideas discussed here and action in the workplace and can make change more likely.

It will help everyone present if you wear your name badge, respect the timetable, and keep mobile telephones and pagers switched off during the sessions.

This is an opportunity to step back from day-to-day operations and consider issues that can help make your job more effective. Be sceptical of your own operation, challenge ideas, remain open-minded throughout and actively seek new thinking that can help you prompt change and improve performance.

Note: here also you may find listed any 'house rules', the observance of which can improve the course experience for everyone attending.

With preparation done, you can move to conducting the session. The next chapter looks at what makes things go well on the day, and Chapter 7 adds some thoughts about participation.

**6**

# Formal training: conducting a session

*Talking and eloquence are not the same: to speak and to speak well are two things.*

*Ben Johnson*

If the last chapter did anything it should have made clear the importance of preparation. This cannot be over-emphasized, and I offer no apologies for starting this chapter with the same thought.

First consider the way in which a message is taken in. Comprehension is not a straightforward process: many things combine to make it more difficult than it might otherwise seem. Surely, if you know your topic there should be no great problem? This is not the case. With communication, difficulties are inherent; more so if you have a serious message that you want to stick in people's memories. Difficulties stem in the main from five areas:

1.  *How people hear:* or rather, how they sometimes do not hear. People find it difficult to concentrate for long periods; their minds flit about (as yours is doing, perhaps, reading

this). This means that messages must be delivered in a way that keeps demanding attention. In addition, people make assumptions about the relative importance of what they hear. They will reject some points, or 'tune out' for a moment if it does not clearly appear to be an important or interesting part of the total message.

2. *How people understand:* understanding is always diluted:
   – if matters are not spelt out clearly or are confused with jargon. Jargon is professional shorthand, useful when everyone knows it to the same degree, confusing if not, and important because using it becomes a habit, one that can take a conscious effort to avoid when necessary;
   – because people misunderstand more easily what they hear but do not see, hence the importance of visual aids;
   – because people draw conclusions ahead of the completion of the message, because they think the ultimate sense is clear to them; and
   – because people make assumptions based on past experience: 'Ah, that's like so and so' they say to themselves, when in fact it isn't, or proves not to be as the full message is spelt out.

3. *How people change their views:* training often involves asking people to change their viewpoint, often a long-held one. This creates suspicion, the same feeling that we sometimes recognize when we deal with someone with 'something to sell'. Additionally, people dislike being proved wrong, and the acceptance of a new view may imply a past mistake in believing something else. Thus communication has to be just right to overcome this factor.

4. *How people decide to act:* change, of course, is a good thing; who wants to be thought of as a 'stick in the mud'? And so it is; but just try going into someone's office tomorrow and saying, 'Right, there are going to be some changes round here, now' and see what response you get. People, for the most part, make changes reluctantly. They do not like changing habits, they are fearful of making

wrong decisions, and of the results of so doing. These are all good reasons for ensuring careful communication.

5. *How feedback occurs:* all the former would be easier if we always knew accurately what was going on and how much of the message was being taken in. But people often hide their reactions, and are protective about what they are thinking, at least in the short term. This is true even to the point where feelings are actively disguised, a nod rather than a 'Yes' in fact indicating puzzlement rather than understanding or agreement.

What is generally happening here is that a message is being filtered as it is received. It is checked for validity, for relevance, to see if it relates to previous experience or clashes with any prejudices, and is then probably only accepted in diluted form. If the communication is good it will get through unscathed, or largely so; if not there are many hazards waiting to make it less effective.

As President Nixon is attributed with saying: 'I know that you understand what you think I said, but I am not sure you realize what you heard is not what I meant.' All this means that the communicator, the manager doing the training in this case, must be careful to communicate in ways that will overcome all, or most, of these difficulties.

Particularly, it is wise to bear in mind the kind of audience you have, especially if in terms of beliefs or experience they are likely to see matters in a way that is different from yourself. You need to make sure that the meaning of what you want to put across is clear; even the wrong or poor choice of one word can change what you want to say. I once heard someone in a presentation describe his organization's 'fragmented range of services'. Whatever he meant (divisionalized for better communication with customers, perhaps), it was the wrong word, and the negative impact on those to whom he was speaking was all too clear. Yet it was just one word; greater confusion will place the message further off target. The danger of jargon, which is also relevant here, has already been mentioned.

Visual aids, which allow you to utilize two senses and add the variety of changing between one and the other, are clearly useful, and it is a rare training event that does not include any. (This was gone into in some detail in the last chapter.)

That's enough of the difficulties, for the moment at least. Let's move to the principles by which learning, which is what we are after, can be made to take place: four approaches help.

# 1. The 'What about me?' factor

Any message is more likely to be listened to and accepted if how it affects people is spelt out. Whatever the effect, in whatever way (and it may be ways) people want to know, 'What's in it for me?' and, 'How will it hurt me?' People are interested in both the potential positive and negative effects. Tell someone that they have to use a new computerized reporting system and they may well think the worst. Certainly their reaction is unlikely to be simply, 'Good for us'; it is more likely to be, 'Sounds like that will be complicated' or, 'Bet that will have teething troubles or take up more time.' Tell them they are going to find it faster and easier to submit returns using the new system. Add that it is already drawing good reactions in another department, and you spell out the message and what the effects on them will be together, rather than leaving them wary or asking questions.

*Whatever you say, bear in mind that people view it in this kind of way. Build in the answers and you avert their potential suspicion and make them more likely to want to take the message on board.*

## 2. The 'That's logical' factor

The sequence and structure of communication is very important. If people know what it is, understand why it was chosen and believe it will work *for them*, then they will pay more attention. Conversely, if it is unclear or illogical then they worry about it, and this takes their mind off listening. Something like this book is an example: it might be possible to have a chapter investigating assessing training effectiveness up front, and a reason for it; but I doubt it (here it comes logically last). Certainly readers would query it and look for a good reason.

Information is remembered and used in an order – you only have to try saying your own telephone number as quickly backwards as you do forwards to demonstrate this – so your selection of a sensible order for communication will make sense to people, and again they will warm to the message. Using an appropriate sequence helps gain understanding and makes it easier for people to retain and use information.

Telling people what you are going to say is called 'flagging' or 'signposting'. Say, 'Let me give you some details about what the reorganization is, when the changes will come into effect and how we will all gain from it' and, provided that makes sense to your staff, they will *want* to hear what comes next. So tell them about the reorganization and then move on. It is almost impossible to overuse signposting. It can lead into a message, giving an overview, and also separately lead into subsections of that message. Sometimes it can be strengthened by explaining why the order has been chosen – 'Let's go through it chronologically, perhaps I could spell out ...', within the phrase.

*Whatever you have to say, think about what you say first, second, third and so on and make the order you choose an appropriate sequence for the staff to whom you are speaking.*

# 3. The 'I can relate to that' factor

Imagine being asked to describe a wonderful sunset. What do you think of? Well, a sunset, you may say. But how do you do this? You recall sunsets you have seen in the past and what you imagine draws on that memory, conjuring up what is probably a composite based on many memories. Because it is reasonable to assume that you have seen a sunset, and enjoyed the experience, in the past, I can be fairly certain that a brief description will put what I want in your mind.

It is, in fact, almost impossible not to allow related things to come into your mind as you take in a message (try it now, and *do not* think about, say, your favourite ice cream. See.) This fact about the way the human mind works must be allowed for and used to promote clear understanding.

On the other hand, if I was to ask you to call to mind, say, the house in which I live and not describe it to you at all, then this is impossible; at least unless you have been there or discussed the matter with me previously. All you can do is guess, wildly perhaps – all authors live in a garret – all authors are rich and live in mansions – (and here this is wrong on both counts!).

So, with this factor also inherent in communication and thus in training, it is useful to try to judge carefully people's prior experience; or indeed to ask about it if they have not worked for you for long and you are unsure of their past experience. You may also refer to it with phrases linking what you are saying to the experience of the other person. For example, saying things like, 'This is like ...', 'You will remember ...', 'Do you know ...?' and 'This is similar, but' are all designed to help the listener grasp what you are saying more easily and more accurately.

*Beware of getting at cross-purposes because you think someone has a frame of reference for something which they do not; link to their experience and use it to reinforce your message.*

## 4. The 'Again and again' factor

Repetition is a fundamental help to grasping a point. Repetition is a fundamental help to …. Sorry. It is true, but it does not imply just saying the same thing, in the same words, repeatedly. Repetition takes a number of forms:

■ things repeated in different ways (or at different stages of the overall message);
■ points made in more than one manner: for example, being spoken and on a slide;
■ using summaries or checklists to recap key points;
■ reminders over a period of time (maybe varying the method: phone, memo or meeting).

This can be overdone (as in the introduction to this point here), but it is also a genuinely valuable aid to getting the message across, especially when used with the other factors now mentioned. People really are more likely to retain what they take in more than once. Enough repetition.

That said, what makes for a good training presentation? There is one overriding factor: empathy, the ability to put yourself in the shoes of participants. Most of what makes people say, 'That's a good presenter' is down to this in one way or another. There is no academic measure – a good presentation is one that the audience like, and in a business context find useful, and in training, of course, it is one from which they learn (preferably something of value) in an interesting way.

So we must think about how we see the audience (the group of trainees), and how they see us. As the latter is more straightforward, let us start with that.

# The way the group think of you

Any trainer must direct the group, must be in charge, and must therefore look the part. There are some who hold that the trainer should always wear a suit, or the equivalent in terms of formality for a woman. There is some sense in this, though it must relate to organizational culture, and while there are no doubt exceptions, the relative positioning of the trainer with the group is usually important. Similarly, stand up as opposed to sitting. (There may be some sessions that can be run while sitting, but not many. Not only does standing influence your profile, but also most trainers will actually perform in a different and more stimulating manner when standing – it heightens the adrenalin.) If standing is the chosen option, stand up straight, do not move about too much, and present an appearance of purposefulness.

The trainer is the expert, is, or should be, in charge, and so appearance is a relevant factor. So too is your apparent confidence and ... what happens when you open your mouth.

# How to think of the group

How you view the group is not, of course, simply a visual point. What is necessary is an understanding of the group, and the individuals in it, and an appreciation of their point of view and their way of seeing things. Training demands decisions of people. 'Do I agree?', 'Can I see the relevance of this?', 'Shall I agree with this point?' So it is necessary to understand the thinking process that takes place in the minds of those in the group in such circumstances.

This thinking follows a common sense sequence of seven stages (and here I paraphrase a much documented approach first developed by psychologists in the United States). All are important to how a message is received, and a successful training session will incorporate them all. Let's review these stages to illustrate how they affect what must be done.

# 1. I am important

We all regard ourselves as important, and what is more we want others to recognize this importance. Unless the trainer is seen to respect members of the group, real learning will not take place. This process must occur directly in terms of normal courtesies, and in terms of the way in which the jobs, responsibilities and performance of people are referred to.

# 2. Consider my needs

That is, needs in terms of what people feel as individuals, and relative to the jobs they do (clearly, these are sometimes in conflict, as with something that will improve job performance but be difficult for the individual); both aspects are important. Attention will always be greater and more immediate if you make it absolutely clear how what is being presented relates to people's needs.

# 3. Will your ideas help me?

If what is being said is beginning to be seen as relevant and useful, then an analysis takes place, in which people ask if it is actually something to accept and implement, either literally or in some modified form. Will it, in fact, work for them?

# 4. What are the facts?

With much of what will be discussed at training sessions, participants are not making snap judgements, though sometimes this will tend to happen, but are intent on *weighing up* the case to see whether they are convinced. They therefore want to know the facts, and they want them logically presented in a form that assists the weighing up process. They ask themselves whether they have enough information, the right information, and whether they are clear about it – do they understand to a degree that will allow the lesson, whatever it is, to be implemented?

## 5. What are the snags?

There are always two sides to any argument. The phrase 'weighing up' used above was deliberately chosen; this is exactly what is happening. Members of the group will ask themselves both what are the reasons to accept this, and what are the points against? Often there are snags, but they do not necessarily rule out acceptance – on balance, they conclude, the case is good. Such snags perceived in this way need either to be anticipated and commented upon to redress the balance included in the presentation or, if reservations come up as questions, they need to be handled effectively with the same aim in mind. It is unrealistic to think that no objections will be raised.

## 6. What shall I do?

Here the process of implementation is also in play. In other words, having weighed up the case – assessed the balance – a participant not only needs to be able to say, 'I accept that point', or even, 'I accept that point and will do it'; they also need to be able to say, 'I accept that, I will do it and I can see how to do it.' The last point is important. How many good ideas are never implemented because people are not sure how to go about it? This is especially true of anything that has about it some genuine difficulty. To paraphrase G K Chesterton, who was writing about Christianity, it is not that some problems are tried and found wanting, it is that they are difficult and therefore not tried.

# 7. I accept

The entire thinking process outlined above will only conclude positively if the process has been allowed, indeed encouraged, to proceed in this manner and sequence. What it is setting out is what people like to do, to some extent what their inherent reaction is to do. If it is going to happen, then we have to work with it and use it to advantage.

Now remembering this, one of the dangers is at once apparent. This is the other person's point of view, and the trainer is as likely to focus on his or her own point of view as anyone else's. You should ensure that you do not become introspective, concerned primarily with your own views or situation. Instead, you use and display enough empathy to come over as constantly concerned about their view. This sounds obvious, but it is all too easy to find your perspective predominating, thus suffering a dilution of effectiveness. Even the most important message has to earn a hearing, and this is achieved primarily through concentrating on what is important to the group. Nervousness of the actual process of presenting training may compound this potential danger.

Next we turn to the structure of the presentation itself, and review how one goes through it. Probably the most famous of all maxims about any kind of communication is the old saying: 'Tell 'em, tell 'em, tell 'em'. This can be stated more clearly as meaning that you should tell people what you are going to tell them, tell them, and then tell them what it was you told them. This sounds silly, perhaps, but compare it with something a little different: the way a good report is set out, for instance. There is an introduction, which says what it is that follows; there is the main body of the document, which goes progressively through the message; and the summary, which, well, summarizes or says what has been covered. The sequence is straightforward, but if it is ignored, messages may then go largely to waste.

So, practising to some degree what I preach, we now split the presentation into three sections, and see not only how to make each effective, but how to ensure that the three together make a satisfactory whole.

# The shape of the presentation

Having said there are three stages – which we review under the more businesslike headings of the beginning, the middle and the end – we start with another, which is either confusing or an example of an intriguing opening. In any case, it has been referred to before – preparation.

Here I wish only to emphasize the point. Preparation is important; as Mark Twain once said, 'It usually takes me three weeks to prepare a good impromptu speech.' If he was half as a good a speaker as he was a writer, then it makes a point. The need for preparation has been referred to in an earlier chapter; however, it should be borne in mind as you read on. We shall now start, with appropriate logic, at the beginning, and see how each stage can be made effective.

## Stage 1: the beginning

The beginning is clearly an important stage. People are uncertain; they are saying to themselves, 'What will this be like?', 'Will I find it interesting; helpful?' They may also have their minds on other matters; what is going on back at their office, the job they left half-finished, how will they cope on their return when they are away even for a day or two? This is particularly true when the people in the group do not know you. They have no previous experience of what to expect, and this conditions their thinking (it is also possible, of course, that previous experience might make them wary!). With people you know well there is less of a problem, but the first moments of any session or programme are nevertheless always important.

It is not only important to the participants, it is also important to the trainer. Nothing settles the nerves – and even the most experienced speakers usually have a few qualms before they start – better than having a good start. Remember, the beginning is, necessarily, the introduction; the main objective is therefore to set the scene, state the topic (and rationale for it) clearly, and begin to discuss the 'meat' of the content. In addition, you have to obtain the group's attention – they will never learn if they are not concentrating and taking in what goes on – and create some sort of rapport both with and around the group. Let us take those aspects in turn.

## Gaining attention

This is primarily achieved by your manner, your confidence and the start you make. You have to look the part, your manner has to say, 'This will be interesting, this person knows what they are talking about.' A little has been said about such factors as appearance, standing up, and so on. Suffice it to say here that if your start appears hesitant, the wrong impression will be given and, at worst, everything thereafter will be more difficult.

More important is what you first say and how it is said. There are a number of types of opening, each presenting a range of opportunities for differing lead-ins. For example:

■ *A question:* rhetorical or otherwise, preferably something that people are likely to respond to positively: 'Would you welcome a better way to ...?'

■ *A quotation:* which might be humorous or make a point, which might be a classic, or novel phrase; or it might be something internal: 'At the last AGM, the MD said ...'.

■ *A story:* again, something that makes a point, relates to the situation or people, or draws on a common memory: 'We all remember the situation at the end of last financial year when ...'.

▦ A *factual statement*: perhaps striking, thought-provoking, challenging or surprising: 'Do you realize that this company receives 120 complaints every working day?' (The fact that this is also a question indicates that all these methods and more can be linked.)

▦ A *dramatic statement*: a story with a startling end, perhaps, or a statement that surprises in some way. For example, in talking about direct mail advertising, I sometimes start by asking the group to count, out loud and in unison, from 1 to 10. Between the count of two and three I bang my fist down on the table saying, 'Stop!' loudly. 'And that,' I continue, 'is how long your direct mail has to catch people's attention – 2½ seconds!'

▦ *An historical fact*: a reference back to an event that is a common experience of the group: 'In 2005, when company sales for what was then a new product were just ...'.

▦ A *curious opening*: simply a statement sufficiently odd for people to want to find out what on earth it is all about: 'Consider the aardvark, and how it shares a characteristic of some of our managers ...'. (In case you want a link, it is thick-skinned.)

▦ A *checklist*: perhaps a good start when placing the 'shopping list' in mind early on is important: 'There are 10 key stages to the process we want to discuss, first ...'.

There must be more methods and combinations of methods that you can think of: whatever you pick, this element of the session needs careful, and perhaps more precise, preparation.

## Creating rapport

At the same time, you need to ensure that an appropriate group feeling is started. In terms of what you say (participation also has a role here, more of this anon), you may want to set a pattern of 'we' rather than 'them and us'; in other words, say 'We need to consider ...' and not, 'You must ...'. If this approach is followed then a more comfortable atmosphere is created. You may add – discreetly – a compliment or two ('As experienced people, you will ...'); mention some common interest; mention some point to verify your competence in the area under discussion ('As an engineer myself ...'), though without overt boasting – and, above all, be enthusiastic. It is said that the one good aspect of life that is infectious is enthusiasm. Use it.

At the same time, the opening stages need to make it absolutely clear what the objectives are, what will be dealt with, and how it will benefit those present. It must also move us into the topic in a constructive way.

This opening stage is the first 'Tell 'em' from 'Tell 'em, tell 'em, tell 'em', and directs itself at the first two stages of the group's seven-stage thinking process referred to earlier.

# Stage 2: The middle

The middle is the core of the session. The objectives are clear:

▨ review of the content in detail;
▨ maintain attention;
▨ ensure acceptance of the message; and
▨ anticipate, prevent and, if necessary, handle any objections.

One of the principles here is to take one point at a time; so I shall do just that.

### Putting over the content

The main trick here is to adopt a structured approach. Make sure you are dealing with points in a *logical sequence*; for instance, working through a process in a chronological order. And use what was referred to as 'flagging', that is straight back to the three 'tell 'ems'. You cannot say something like, 'There are three key points here: performance, method and cost; let's deal with them in turn. First, performance ...'; too much. Giving advance warning of what is coming, putting it in context, and relating it to a planned sequence, keeps the message organized and improves understanding.

This technique, and consistent clarity give you the overall effect you want. People must obviously understand what you are talking about. There is no room for verbosity, for too much jargon, or for anything that might cloud understanding. A pretty good measure of the trainer is when people feel afterwards that, perhaps for the first time, they really have come to understand something clearly.

You cannot refer to manual excavation devices; in training a spade has to be called a spade. What is more, it has, as it were, to be an interesting and relevant spade if attention is to be maintained.

## Maintaining attention

Some of the factors that are important here link with topics reviewed elsewhere. The principles are straightforward.

Keep stressing the relevance of what is being discussed to the participants. For instance, do not only say that some change will be a cost saving to the organization; stress personal benefits – will it make something easier, quicker or more satisfying to do, perhaps?

Make sure that the presentation remains visually interesting by using visual aids and demonstrations.

Use descriptions that incorporate stories or anecdotes to make the message live. You cannot have too many anecdotes, and if your memory is less than perfect you will need a method of recording them and, just as important, accessing them.

Involve people, a topic investigated at some length in the next chapter. As well as the techniques for creating participation reviewed there, it is necessary to have a participative attitude. The best trainers appear to digress, and take questions and involve people in a variety of unplanned ways; yet they still finish on time, having dealt with the published content.

Finally, continue to generate attention through your own interest and enthusiasm.

## Obtaining acceptance

People will only implement what they have come to believe is good sense. It is not enough to have put the message over and have it understood: it has to be believed.

Here we must start by going back to understanding; nothing will be truly accepted unless this is achieved. To recap – understanding is helped by:

■ Using clear, precise language – language which is familiar to those present and which does not over-use jargon.
■ Making explanation clear, making no assumptions, using plenty of similes (you can hardly say 'This is like ...' too often), and with sufficient detail to get the point across. One danger here is that in explaining points that you know well, you start to abbreviate, allowing your understanding to blind you as to how far back it is necessary to go with people for whom the message is new.
■ Demonstrations add considerably to the chances of understanding. These can be specific: product knowledge training can include an object lesson in assembling something, for instance. In this case, the golden rule is (surprise, surprise) preparation. Credibility is immediately at risk if a demonstration does not work first time and in a straightforward manner. Alternatively, a physical, visual demonstration may make a different point, like having someone describe how to tie a necktie to show the difficulty of voice-only communication, as in telephone skills training.
■ Visual aids are a powerful tool in promoting understanding. As the old saying has it, 'A picture is worth a thousand words.' Graphs are an excellent example of this:

many people instantly understand a point from a clear graph, which would usually elude them in a mass of figures. (Visual aids have been commented on elsewhere.)

It is not, however, just a question of understanding. As has been said, acceptance is also vital. Acceptance is helped by factors already mentioned (telling people how something will benefit them – or others they are concerned about, such as their colleagues or staff), and the more specific this link can be made the better the effect will be on the view formed.

In addition, acceptance may only come once validity has been established and this, in turn, may demand something other than your saying, in effect, 'This is right.' Validity can be improved by references, what other people say. A description that shows how well an idea or system has worked in another department and sets this out chapter and verse may be a powerful argument. As always with references, this is dependent on the source of the reference being respected. If the other department is regarded in a negative way, then its adopting some process or product may be regarded by others as being a very good reason not to have anything to do with it. References work best when the results of what is being quoted are included so that the message says they did this and so and so has occurred since, with sufficient detail to make it interesting and credible.

Finally, it is worth making the point that you will not always know whether acceptance of a point has been achieved, at least not without checking. People cannot be expected to nod or speak out at every point, yet knowing that you have achieved acceptance may be important as you proceed. Questions to establish appropriate feedback are therefore a necessary part of this process. It is also advisable to keep an eye on the visible signs, watching, for instance, for puzzled looks.

## Handling objections

The first aspect here is the anticipation, indeed the pre-emption, of objections. On occasions it is clear that some subject to be dealt with is likely, even guaranteed, to produce a negative reaction. If there is a clear answer then it can be built into the presentation, avoiding any waste of time. It may be as simple as a comment such as, 'Of course, this needs time, always a scarce resource, but once set up time will be saved; regularly', which then goes on to explain how this will happen. Otherwise, if objections are voiced – and of course they will be – then a systematic procedure is necessary if they are to be dealt with smoothly.

First, give it a moment: too glib an answer may be mistrusted or make the questioner feel – or look – silly. So, pause ... and for long enough to give yourself time to think (which you might just need), and to give the impression of consideration. An acknowledgement reinforces this: 'That's a good point. We must certainly think about that', though be careful of letting such a comment become a reflex and be seen as such. Then you can answer, with either a concentration on the individual's point and perspective, or with a general emphasis that is more useful to the group; or both, in turn.

Very importantly, never, ever bluff. If you do not know the answer you must say so (no group expects you to be infallible), though you may well have to find out the answer later and report back. Alternatively, does anyone else know? Similarly, there is no harm in delaying a reply: 'That's a good point, perhaps I can pick it up, in context, when we deal with ...'. More about questions – 'objections' in any case being too strong a word for some – in the next chapter.

A final word here: beware of digression. It is good to answer any ancillary points that come up, but you can stray too far. Part of the training job is that of chairperson; everything planned has to be covered, and covered before the scheduled finishing time. If, therefore, you have to draw a close to a line of enquiry, and you may well have to do so, make it clear that time is pressing. Do not ever let anyone feel it was a silly point to have raised.

After all this, when we have been through the session, the time comes to conclude.

## Stage 3: The end

Always end on a high note. The group expect it, if only sub-consciously. It is an opportunity to build on past success during the session or, occasionally, to make amends for anything that has been less successful; that apart, the end is a pulling together.

However you finally end, with something as complex as a training session there is nearly always a need to summarize in an orderly fashion. This may well be linked to an action plan for the future, so that in wrapping up what has been reviewed – completing the 'Tell 'ems' – a commitment is sought as to what should happen next. This is important. Most people are under pressure for time and, whatever else, training takes time. They will be busier after even a day or two attending a course than would be the case if they had not attended, so there is a real temptation to put everything on one side and get back to work – get back to normal. Yet this may be just where a little time needs to be put in to start to make some changes. Their having a real intention in mind as they leave the programme is not a guarantee that action will flow, but it is a start, and it makes it that much more likely that something will happen, especially if there is suitable follow-up.

Like the beginning, there is then a need to find a way of handling, in this case, the final signing off. You can, for instance, finish with:

■ *A question:* that leaves the final message hanging in the air, or makes it more likely that people will go on thinking about the issues a little longer: 'I asked a question at the start of the session, now let us finish with another. What ...?'

▨ A *quotation:* that encapsulates an important, or the last, point: 'Good communication is as stimulating as black coffee, and just as hard to sleep after' (Anne Morrow Lingberg). Or, while not linked inextricably to the topic, a good closing line is: 'The more I practise, the more good luck I seem to have' (which is attributed to just about every famous golfer there is).

▨ A *story:* longer than the quotation, but with the same sort of intention. If it is meant to amuse, be sure it does; you have no further chance at the end to retrieve the situation. That said, I will resist the temptation to give an example, though a story close does not only imply a humorous story. *Note:* I have written about the use of humour in training in *Hook your Audience* (Management Pocketbooks).

▨ An *alternative:* this may be as simple, as 'Will you do this or that?', or the more complicated options of a spelt out plan A, B or C.

▨ *Immediate gain:* this is an injunction to act linked to an advantage of doing so now: 'Put this new system in place and you will be saving time and money tomorrow' – more fiercely phrased, it is called a fear-based end: 'Unless you ensure this system is running you will not ...'. The positive route is usually better.

However you decide to wrap things up, the end should be a logical conclusion, rather than something separate added on the end.

All of this has much in common with the skills of any presentation. There is a difference, however. You want people not just to say that they enjoyed your session, you want them to learn from it. The ways in which people learn are therefore important principles to keep in mind throughout. It needs patience as well as intellectual weight or 'clout'. It needs sensitivity to the feedback as well as the ability to come through it. As with many skills, the difficulty is less with the individual elements, most of which are straightforward and common sense, than with the orchestration of the whole process. The trainer must be able to present effectively, to remain flexible throughout, and work with the group rather than talking at them.

Remember a good definition: 'Training is helping people to learn': that means a particular kind of presentation is necessary, one that involves the group and the individuals in it. And this is the ultimate variable. People are inherently unpredictable; you never know quite what is going to happen. Add the management of this to the elements already reviewed, and we are really talking about working a group. This makes it sound like a manipulative process, which in a sense it is – though it should never appear so in any unpleasant way – participation must be constructive if it is to assist learning.

It must be made to happen. There is nothing worse than the uneasy silence that can ensue if no comment, discussion or questions are forthcoming at the appropriate moment. How this aspect is added, seamlessly, to the whole is the subject of the next chapter.

Let us put ourselves into a participative mood – read on.

# 7

# Formal training: the power of participation

What we have to learn to do, we learn by doing.

*Aristotle*

So far so good: the previous chapter looked at straightforward presentation factors. Straightforward, at least, in the sense, that we concentrated on the communication directed from the trainer to the participants. But training demands participation. Without it even the best-presented session can become dull. More important, 'doing' rather than simply listening is more likely to produce both learning and retention, and therefore a subsequent change in behaviour.

This chapter describes a variety of participative techniques. It is not suggested that everything referred to should be used in every session; that would create an 'all singing, all dancing' effect, and total confusion. What is reviewed is more in the nature of a shopping list: you will recognize elements that are necessary in every session, others that are appropriate on an occasional basis.

Participation may need introducing into sessions; if it does there is merit in introducing it early on. We shall start, therefore, logically, at the beginning.

# First impressions last

You only have one chance to make a good first impression. That may be a cliché, but it makes an important point.

As has been said, a course leader is much more than simply a presenter. The job is normally more than imparting knowledge; you have to change behaviour, even attitudes. This may be a difficult job in any case; it will be doubly difficult if you do not have the participants' attention and interest, and obtaining this begins in the first few minutes.

It can even start before the session really begins. You know the awkward moments before start time: you are waiting for the last few attendees to arrive, and – particularly if you are busy with last minute preparations – conversation of those present may flag.

It is quite possible at this stage to start things off without actually starting the programme. For instance, even a simple *instruction*, 'Perhaps you would like to complete the name card in front of you before we start' will create some action. Alternatively, you can use some point to *prompt relevant conversation*; for instance: 'Do introduce yourself to your immediate neighbours' (when they do not know each other, or not well), or 'Do ask your neighbours how they see the programme briefing. What is the most important objective today?' (*Note*: if people do not know each other well, always use name cards so that everyone can address everyone else by name.)

*Always start on time.* You must lead by example in this respect, and running to time is important, not least to you in accordance with your planning. Your starting on time, completing what you intended for a session – in spite of any digressions – and finishing on time help make what you are doing appear more professional. Sometimes this presents problems. I run courses on time management. I always start on time, but sometimes have to have a double start so that any latecomers are included!

So, on time, you begin. Immediately there are conflicting priorities. You need to deal with a variety of administrative points. Some, such as how you plan to handle questions, may be important to mention early on. You also need to come quickly to the 'meat' of the topic in a way that generates interest and rapport.

There is no 'best' sequence. Some trainers prefer to get the administration out of the way before starting on the training content. Some prefer to spend a moment generating interest, then go on to deal with the formalities almost as a digression, before coming back to the content.

The following section presents all the main elements of this stage in a logical order, but it is not the only possible order. You must decide for yourself with a particular session in mind.

A strong start is not only important in itself – it can set the scene for participation, perhaps by involving some people at once through questions, perhaps simply by creating an atmosphere that will make participation easier at a later stage. Some methods described here provide examples of many of these opportunities. Some of the starting methods described in the last chapter are revisited in the box that follows.

## How to start

The first statement may be:

▦ A question (actual or, more likely at this stage, rhetorical): 'Would you be interested in a way of ...'.

- A quotation (attributable): 'Advertising may be described as the science of arresting human intelligence long enough to get money from it', Stephen Leacock.
- A saying (not attributable): 'He is never lost for a few appropriated words.' (Note: carefully chosen quotations or sayings can be a safer way of introducing a slight element of humour than the 'funny story'.)
- A story: 'You may remember what happened when our last new product was launched …'.
- A positive/interesting/arresting fact: 'Sales figures are at record levels.'
- A historic reference: 'In 2000, when the company had achieved a million pound turnover for the first time …'.

Beyond that, welcome the participants to the sessions. Introduce yourself, and explain your role. (If necessary) ask each participant to introduce themselves to the group – specifying exactly how, and how long, this should take. Outline the course objectives, programme, timetable and methodology. This may usefully cover the following.

## Course outline

- *What* you will cover: 'The coverage is …'.
- Perhaps also what you will *not* cover: 'The intention is not to be comprehensive, but to concentrate on key areas …'.
- *How* it will be done: 'As you will have seen from the programme, whilst I shall lead the proceedings, there are exercises for you to do, a training film … and the session will end with some role-play.'
- *How* participation, particularly questions, will be handled: 'I shall take questions and comments as we proceed, so do say if anything is not clear or …'.

> ■ A concise encapsulation of any *administrative* points: 'Let me list quickly some of the admin points ...'. (*Note:* This may include timings, dietary requirements, telephone and message procedures, where the toilets are located, fire precautions, duration of breaks, a word about strict time-keeping, and more.)
>
> ■ *Participants' notes* are often worth a special word, so that people do not spend time writing text that will be issued later: 'I shall let you have a clear résumé note at ...'.
>
> ■ Link what the course is about clearly and positively to the jobs of those present. Not just 'This is important', but 'This is important to you because ...'.

Most training is better received if it can be made motivational, and if it is positioned positively – making things better rather than correcting faults.

# Ice-breakers

In addition, and the exact placing of this is also variable, you may need what is often called an 'ice-breaker' early on. This usually refers to an exercise, which is there simply to kick-start proceedings. It may puzzle, intrigue, and make participants think, or just surprise them. For example, these two are classics:

1. What letter comes next in the sequence O T T F F _____ ?

2. Does F go above or below the line in the following sequence? A_____E__
           B C D

(The answers are at the end of this chapter, on page 126, just in case you need a moment to think!)

The best ice-breakers, however, for any specific occasion, are on a topic, or have a moral, which links to the course content. They can be simple, like the following, which links again to presentations skills.

Ask the participants to draw a circle and divide it pie-chart style into the ratio of the influence of what someone says and what comes over from slides. You can do this for how they operate now and, if different, how they should operate. It prompts useful discussion and, for the record, the majority influence should surely be with the individual.

Alternatively, they can be longer and more complex. For instance, my favourite one involves making teams complete two jigsaw puzzles (with only one of the pictures to guide them), and during just 20/30 minutes demonstrates just about every aspect of leadership and teamwork you care to mention.

A final note. You should have the course well under way by this stage, but remember that your approach, confidence, style and so on are saying a great deal to people in those first few minutes. They go through the first 10 minutes or half an hour saying to themselves, 'What can this person teach me? Can I see myself usefully spending an hour, or a day or two, in their company?'

If you are dealing with a matter of which you have personal experience, it may be desirable to drop into the introductions some point that demonstrates your own competence, some anecdote perhaps – it need not suggest you are the best in the world at whatever it is, but it would suggest that you know your subject well. I have mentioned the saying, 'You don't need to be able to lay eggs to be a chicken farmer', though of course it does help to know the backside from the beak.

We can turn now to the formal, presentational, inputs.

# Getting people involved

There is a story of someone coming home after a course. Their partner asks, 'What was it like?' and they reply, 'It was good, I spoke.' People like to be involved. They can often learn as much from each other, from the thinking generated by questions, discussion, exercises and so on as from the formal inputs. Consider questions first.

## Taking questions

The first decision is when to take questions. This can be seen as a compromise because:

▪ questions allowed at any time can disrupt the planned balance of a presentation – you must exercise control;
▪ delaying questions to the very end can frustrate the group, and give you a false sense of security that the earlier points have been accepted;
▪ discouraging questions, or leaving no time for them, is poor training.

You may therefore plan to take questions after each main point. Whatever you do, tell the group the rules; allow time in the presentation for the chosen methodology to work.

As you handle questions from the group, you may find it useful to use the following techniques:

▪ Acknowledge the question and questioner.
▪ Ensure, as necessary, that the question is heard and understood by the rest of the group.
▪ If in doubt as to what is meant, probe to clarify and restate it back if necessary.
▪ Give short informative answers whenever possible and link to other parts of your message, as appropriate.

■ If you opt, which you may want to, to take questions at any time, remember it is perfectly acceptable to:
  - hold them for a moment until you finish making a point,
  - delay them: saying you will come back to it, in context in, say, the next session (then you must remember: make a note of both the point and who made it),
  - refuse them. Some may be irrelevant or likely to lead to too much of a digression, but be *careful* not to do this too often, to respect the questioner's feelings, and to explain why you are doing so.
■ If you don't know the answer, you *must* say so (and find out or whatever). The fact that no one expects you to be omniscient has been made: if you are well prepared it will not happen very often.

# Asking questions

The questions you ask can check understanding, or prompt discussion, and make the group explore a point, building their understanding. They will retain information better if there is an element of finding out involved in its acquisition rather than only 'being told'.

Questions must be put *precisely*. Witness the apocryphal story of the question, which asks people, 'Are you in favour of smoking whilst praying?' This does not sound very good, and most people will say, 'No'. But ask, 'Are you in favour of praying whilst smoking?' and most will say, 'Yes' (is there a time when one should not pray?). Yet both phrases concern the simultaneous carrying out of two actions. The moral is to be careful to ask the question in the right way, or you may not obtain the answer you want.

Many questions are best phrased as open questions. These cannot be answered yes or no, and so are more likely to prompt discussion. They typically start with: what, why, where, who, how or, in training, can be neatly led into by asking people to:

| | | |
|---|---|---|
| Describe ... | Explain ... | Discuss ... |
| Justify ... | Clarify ... | Illustrate ... |
| Outline ... | Verify ... | Define ... |
| Review ... | Compare ... | Critique ... |

There are several ways of directing questions. They can be:

■ *Overhead questions*, put to the group generally, and useful for opening up a subject (if there is no response, then you can move on to the next method): 'Right, what do you think the key issue here is? Anyone?'

■ *Overhead and then directed at an individual*, useful to make the whole group think before looking for an answer from one person: 'Right, what do you think the key issue here are? Anyone? ... John, what do you think?'

■ *Direct to individual*, useful for obtaining individual responses, testing for understanding: 'John, what would you do?'

■ *Non-response/rhetorical*, useful where you want to make a point to one or more people in the group without concentrating on anyone in particular, or for raising a question you would expect to be in the group's mind and then answering it yourself: 'What's the key issue? Well, perhaps it's ...'.

All these methods represent very controlled discussion, ie, leader to team member to leader to another team member (or more), then ... back to the leader. Two other types of question help to open up a discussion:

■ *Redirected questions*, useful to make others in the group answer any individual's answer: 'That's a good point John. What do you think the answer is, Mary?'

■ *Developmental questioning*, where you take the answer to a previous question and move it around the audience, building on it: 'Having established that, how about ...?'

Whichever of the above is being used, certain principles should be borne in mind. For questioning to be effective, the following general method may be a useful guide to the kind of sequence that can be employed:

1. *State the question clearly and concisely.* Questions should relate directly to the subject being discussed. Whenever possible they should require people to think, to draw on their past experiences, and relate them to the present circumstances.
2. *Ask the question first to the group rather than to an individual.* If the question is directed to a single individual, others are off the hook and do not have to think about the answer. Direct, individual questions are more useful to break a general silence in the group, or to involve someone who is not actively participating in the discussion.
3. *After asking the question, pause ...* Allow a few moments for the group to consider what the answer should be. Then:
4. *Ask a specific individual to answer.* This four-step process starts the entire group thinking because they never know who will be called on. Thus everyone has to consider each question you ask, and be ready to participate. Even those who are not called on are still involved.

To be sure of using an effective questioning technique, note some points which should be avoided, such as:

■ *Asking yes or no questions.* Participants can attempt to guess the answer (and may be right). Such questions should not be used if you want participants to use their reasoning power and actively participate in the training.
■ *Asking tricky questions.* Remember, your purpose is to train people, not to antagonize them or make them look bad. Difficult questions, yes. Tricky, no. Keep personalities and sarcasm out of your questions.
■ *Asking unanswerable questions.* You want to provide

knowledge, not confusion. Be sure that the knowledge and experience of your group are such that at least some participants can answer the questions you ask. Never attempt to highlight ignorance by asking questions that the group can't handle. This is particularly true when you're trying to draw out a silent trainee and involve them. Be sure they can answer before you ask them the questions.

▓ *Asking personal questions.* Personal questions are usually rather sensitive, even in one-to-one sessions. They are often inappropriate in a group session.

▓ *Asking leading questions.* This is where the trainer indicates the preferred answer in advance: 'Mary, don't you agree that this new form will help solve the problem?' Such questions require little addition; even if Mary didn't agree, she would probably be uncomfortable saying so. After all, that does not seem to be the answer you want.

▓ *Repeating questions.* Don't make a practice of repeating the question for an inattentive person. Doing so simply encourages further inattention and wastes valuable time. Instead, ask someone else to respond. People will quickly learn that they have to listen.

▓ *Allowing group answers.* Unless written down (and then referred to around the group), questions that allow several members of the group to answer are not useful. First, everyone cannot talk at once. Second, with group answers a very few participants may well tend to dominate the session. And third, group answers allow the silent person to hide and not participate as he or she should.

*Note:* one unbreakable rule that all training sessions should have, clearly understood and adhered to, is: only one person may talk at once (and the leader must be the acknowledged referee and decide who has the floor at any particular moment.

Above all, let your questioning be natural. Ask because you want to know – because you want this information to be shared with the group. Never think of yourself as a quizmaster with certain questions that must be asked whether or not they're timely. Let your manner convey your interest in the response you're going to get, and be sure that your interest is genuine. Forced artificial enthusiasm will never fool a group.

No matter how effective your questioning technique may become, never consider yourself so clever that you can manipulate the participants. Manipulation is not its purpose. Instead, questioning should be used to promote and build genuine participation, not to bend the group to your will.

Finally, for questioning to be an effective instructional technique you must create the proper atmosphere in which it can flourish. For example, participants should never fear to give an incorrect answer. If wrong answers are discouraged, participants will respond more cautiously. In addition, people should never have the feeling that they are asking stupid questions. It cannot be over-emphasized that they should be encouraged to ask questions, at any time, about anything they do not understand.

# Using exercises

Questions can prompt discussion, which is valuable in two ways: people like, and learn from, participation as a process; and the discussion may well be creative, casting new light on some aspect of the subject. However, people will learn still more from actually working at a task.

Exercises can be as short as a few minutes or as long as many hours. For the purposes of the present discussion, which relates primarily to short training sessions of perhaps three hours to three days, exercises can be conducted in several ways:

■ *Individually:* there is a place for participants individually working through an exercise; one benefit is that of letting people work at their own pace, and on their own situations or problems. Protracted individual exercises in a group situation can seem inappropriate, and are therefore best kept short. Some topics make some use of them – I always spend some individual time on business writing courses – but it needs the right balance.

■ *In pairs:* working in pairs gives some of the advantages of individual exercises, yet involves active participation. It is affected by room layout, and works best when people are seated so they can simply turn to their neighbours and go straight into an exercise without moving. (Additionally, an individual exercise can then be commented on, or developed, in pairs.)

■ *In syndicates:* working in syndicates takes somewhat longer, and may involve some moving about, but it is useful. There should not be too many in a group, five to eight perhaps, and you can make it work best by suggesting that:

   – a chairperson is promptly selected (or nominated) to control discussion and keep an eye on the time;
   – a 'recorder' is chosen to keep notes of points agreed;
   – a presenter is chosen to report back to the main group.

If each exercise has a different chairperson or presenter, everyone is given an active role as syndicate sessions progress, and tasks are spread round the group.

The ultimate form of exercise, particularly for training in interactive skills (selling, communication, interviewing, counselling, etc) is role-playing. This needs careful setting up, and is worth considering in more detail before we move on.

# Making role-playing effective

Role-playing is a very powerful technique, though not necessarily the easiest activity to organize. If role-playing is to be valuable it needs to be used carefully. It provides practice in a 'safe' environment: if you are practising selling, interviewing or presentational techniques, for instance, it avoids upsetting real customers, applicants or audiences.

At its simplest, role-playing is just the informal enactment of a real-life situation. Say you are training in interviewing skills. You pose a question that leads into conversation: 'Imagine the applicant says ...' (and you quote). 'What would you reply?' This question, directed at one of the participants with an injunction to reply *verbatim*, creates a moment of conversation: one that can either be between you and the participant, or between two participants. These conversations carry on between the two parties for a moment or two, or for a few minutes, and then the session returns to normal. This is role-playing. People are made to think about the topic, not in academic terms, but very much in its day-to-day application. Yet there is no formality, none of the equipment, recording and playback more normally associated with role-playing.

At the other end of the scale there is considerable formality, with all the panoply of equipment and recording, which can be daunting. For example, I have been involved in role-playing that returns in four main sessions during one day to the same developing scenario, or which even uses people from outside the course and the organization (this, for example, in training in recruitment interviewing skills, where real interviews with actual candidates have been filmed – with the permission of the candidates – to assist in developing key skills). So, elaborate forms are certainly possible, and can work well.

To return to the more routine, and start with the dangers, role-playing can fail and, if it does, the cause probably lies among the following:

- ▪ over-awareness of the camera;
- ▪ over-acting to the camera;
- ▪ a belief that role-playing means acting;

▓ the difficulty of 'performing' in front of one's peers;
▓ poor role-play briefs;
▓ weak management of the role-play;
▓ incomplete or unconstructive feedback after the role-play;
▓ those not role-playing being given nothing to do.

Most positively, all role-plays should be organized to achieve one or more of the following objectives:

▓ reproduce real life as closely as possible;
▓ provide an opportunity to practise difficult situations;
▓ provide an opportunity to practise new skills;
▓ develop confidence;
▓ enhance learning by building on success;
▓ experiment with new approaches;
▓ change negative habits/reinforce positive habits;
▓ fix knowledge and an attitude of professionalism;
▓ promote analytical skill through self-appraisal and observing others.

The following details four different forms of role-playing which, although these can be adapted, amended and used in a variety of different ways, make useful examples, and show how to make role-playing work well and generate constructive feedback. Though I have described them in terms of video use, there is no reason why they should not be effective without this facility.

## The 'classic' role-play

This is where two participants act out a situation to reinforce an interactive skill. Assuming a clear objective, and the use of standard video equipment (ie, camera/tripod, microphone, video recorder and TV monitor), the physical arrangements must be able to comfortably facilitate what needs to take place.

Though, of course, no one sequence of events should be followed slavishly, the following illustrates a typical approach:

1. Issue the role-play briefs to the two participants, and allow them time to plan their approaches. If either is playing themselves this should be made clear. It is certainly less confusing if participants use their own names, whatever their roles.
2. State the objectives, and summarize the briefs for the observers.
3. Issue any observation and feedback forms to the observers. (A specific, sales training, example appears in the boxed example overleaf; a simple rating scale can help here).
4. Emphasize that theirs is an active role in the learning process.
5. Introduce the camera operator (if one is used). Brief them on what they should capture on film, ie, one participant's role, the other's reactions or both.
6. Indicate when you want the role-play to end, say after a certain time, or when a particular point in the content has been reached.
7. Invite questions, checking that everyone knows what to do.
8. Emphasize that a role-play is a group learning exercise, not an opportunity to test one individual.
9. Invite the two role-players to take their places. (Layout needs some thought: role-players need to be away from distractions, and any equipment conveniently positioned.)
10. Take your seat near the video deck, and be prepared to note down the running numbers of where key points occur during the exchanges.

When the role-play has finished:

1. Thank the two participants and invite them to rejoin the group.

2. Ask the observers to complete their feedback notes.
3. Ask the two participants to write down their own impressions of their experience.
4. Allow the lead player to comment first, drawing in the other as appropriate.
5. Ask the observers to offer their initial impressions.
6. Offer your own initial impressions.
7. Play back the opening moments of the role-play, using this as your cue to lead a discussion on particular details.
8. Ensure that the observers' feedback is constructive, and the participants are allowed to respond.
9. Use the video to highlight key points.
10. At an appropriate point, draw the discussions to a close. Ask for final comments from the observers; invite final comments from the participants and then summarize.

## Example: Observation and feedback form

Participants: Salesperson: _____  Customer _____
Role-play objective: _____

| | A+ | A | B+ | B |
|---|---|---|---|---|
| How well did the salesperson listen to the customer? | [ ] | [ ] | [ ] | [ ] |
| How well did the salesperson's replies satisfy the customer? | [ ] | [ ] | [ ] | [ ] |
| How clear and understandable were the salesperson's questions? | [ ] | [ ] | [ ] | [ ] |
| How well did the salesperson control the interview? | [ ] | [ ] | [ ] | [ ] |

What was the salesperson's level of
product knowledge?                           [ ]  [ ]  [ ]  [ ]

What was the salesperson's level of
competitor product knowledge?               [ ]  [ ]  [ ]  [ ]

How well did the salesperson use his or
her sales aids?                              [ ]  [ ]  [ ]  [ ]

How well did the salesperson spot
and use opportunities to conclude the
interview positively?                        [ ]  [ ]  [ ]  [ ]

General impressions: _____

_____

Recommendations: _____

_____

Your summary should be divided into distinct elements: thanks and praise for the participants; thanks for the observers; summarizing the key learning points which first, directly affect the individual(s), and second, may apply to the group.

Rewind the tape and prepare for the next role-play.

# The 'carousel' role-play

This role-play involves the situation being started by two participants and, at an appropriate point, being handed over to two others, who continue to act out the same scenario. It is thus a good way of involving more people in the group, more quickly.

Again, a typical but not definitive sequence of events illustrates what is involved:

1.  Divide the complete process into suitable parts (eg, a sales interview might be divided into the opening, establishing needs, presenting the product/service, handling objections, and gaining a commitment. An interview, more simply, might be organized into a beginning, a middle and the conclusion). Ensure that the group understands the basis for the split.
2.  Divide the group into pairs (this might just be progressively around a U-shaped seating plan), and nominate who in each pair will play which role. However, do *not* indicate the part of the sequence that each pair will play, not least so that everyone will concentrate throughout the proceedings.
3.  Distribute the carousel role-play instructions (see the boxed example overleaf).
4.  Distribute any necessary role-play briefs. (*Note:* all members of the group should be given the same two briefs, one for each of the roles.)
5.  Invite or nominate two participants to play the first interview phase.
6.  Begin the role-play.
7.  At an appropriate point, stop the role-play and either invite a second pair to continue from that point, or play back and take feedback comments, then invite a second pair to continue.
8.  When the complete scenario has been role-played, lead a feedback discussion in the same way as for the 'classic' role-play. This can be simply done, even without video.

# Carousel role-playing instructions

## *Objectives*

To reinforce skill at

To actively involve everyone

One of our typical interviews has been broken down into its key phases:

(i) _____    (iii) _____

(ii) _____    (iv) _____

Each pair will role-play one of these phases.

You all will have a copy of the same two briefs, one for each role.

The first pair will role-play the first interview phase. At an appropriate point their role-play will be stopped and a second pair will be invited to *continue the interview without losing its direction and building upon what has already been established.* This pair will role-play the second interview phase.

Again, at an appropriate point this role-play will be stopped and a third pair will be invited to *continue the same interview, also without losing direction and building upon the facts and agreements already established.* Their task is to role-play the third interview phase.

*You must remain alert*, listening and taking notes so that, whenever it is your turn to take over you are able to *maintain the interview momentum.*

Throughout the interview you may introduce new information. However, if you do, this must:

> ■ not be designed to 'catch out' the other 'player';
> ■ not directly contradict whatever has already been established
>   and agreed;
> ■ sensibly reflect real-life situations.
>
> The role-play will continue until a clear conclusion has been
> reached.
>
> The trainer may temporarily halt the role-play between pairs
> either to play back the video recording or to summarize key
> agreements between the two parties.

## The 'silent' role-play

This sort of role-play is 'silent' because the scenario is enacted
in writing. This is clearly unsuited to anything lengthy, but is
very valuable when great precision is necessary (eg, the brief
moments when a prospecting salesperson introduces his or her
company on the telephone; the summary in a discipline interview where the wording must be exactly right). Again, a typical
sequence of events illustrates the process:

1.  Divide the group into pairs, and brief them about their
    respective roles. Check that all is clear.
2.  Then a conversation is acted and written down – word for
    word. This is done on the same sheet of paper – passed
    between the two – so that the developing conversation
    remains visible in its entirety.
3.  Once the exchanges are complete the whole conversation
    can be read out and discussed. (*Note:* This also works well
    with the trainer playing one role and inter-relating with
    individual members of the group; and also with syndicates
    discussing, and noting, a measured response.)

4. There should be no (out of role) talking between parties during the role-play.
5. The real learning will take place during and after role-play; it teaches the importance of thinking about, clearly expressing and logically structuring what you want to say. Seeing the actual words in black and white can be an object lesson in learning how to focus and clarify spoken presentations.

## The 'triad' role-play

As the name suggests, this involves three people participating in three roles during the role-play session (eg, an appraisal meeting at which a subordinate, a manager and an observer – perhaps a personnel person – is present).

This can either work very like the 'classic' role-play, or the third person can be an observer (but act 'in character'); thus, the role-play observer's task is to observe, then comment upon the two role-play participants. (Essentially, he or she plays the trainer.)

The remainder of the group have a dual task: to comment on the role-play participants; and to watch and comment on the observer's analysis.

After the first round of the role-play, the observer moves into participant A's seat, and A moves to the other side of the table and becomes B. B rejoins the group, and a new player takes over as observer (ie, an element of carousel).

The trainer's role is to orchestrate the action and learning, not forgetting that the emphases in this type of role-playing are: the participants and the skills displayed, and the observer and their analysis and appraisal skills.

From the least formal format, mentioned earlier, to the more complex, role-playing is an important tool of training. It should not, however, be underestimated in terms of the care and preparation it necessitates. If it moves off track, if it goes badly, then people are made to look inadequate which, understandably, they do not like. Provided participants are clear as to the brief, and understand the purpose of the exercise, and provided that the trainer sets up the situation carefully and makes it a risk-free experience, it can add to a training session to a meaningful extent. Its greatest contribution is not in providing a test of individuals, but in creating discussion of examples and situations, which the whole group can use, and from which approaches for the future can be constructed.

Finally in such sessions, you should recognize that not all the people in any group are the same. Everyone is an individual, everyone responds to the group situation differently; but you have to work with them all.

# Different people

As someone once observed, training would be easy if it were not for the participants. Whilst all are understandably different, some present problems. These problems must be tackled firmly, if only because by their attitude or characteristics people may not only fail to learn as much themselves as you would wish, they may also disrupt things for other members of the group.

The following snapshots suggest cures designed to direct problem participants – tactfully – back to the discussion at hand:

■ The 'show off'. Avoid embarrassing or shutting them off; you may need their participation later. *Solution:* toss them a difficult question. Or say, 'That's an interesting point. Let's see what the group thinks of it.'
■ The 'quick reactor'. Can also be valuable later, but can keep others out of the discussion. *Solution:* thank them, suggest we put others to work.

■ The 'heckler'. This one argues about every point being made. *Solution:* remain calm. Agree, affirm any good points but toss bad points to the group for discussion. They will be quickly rejected. Privately try to find out what's bothering them, try to elicit their cooperation.

■ The 'rambler'. Talks about everything except the subject under discussion. *Solution:* at a pause in their monologue, thank them, return to and restate the relevant points of the discussion, and go on.

■ The 'mutual enemies', where there is a clash of personalities. *Solution:* emphasize points of agreement, minimize differences. Or frankly ask that personalities be left out. Draw attention back to the point being made.

■ The 'pig-headed'. Absolutely refuses, perhaps through prejudice, to accept points being discussed. *Solution:* throw their points to the group, and have them straighten them out. Say time is short, that you'll be glad to discuss it with them later.

■ The 'digresser', who takes the discussion too far off track. *Solution:* take the blame yourself. Say, 'Something I said must have led you off the subject, this is what we should be discussing …'.

■ The 'professional gripe', who makes frankly political points. *Solution:* politely point out that we cannot change policy here; the objective is to operate as best we can under the present system. Or better still, have a member of the group answer him or her.

■ The 'whisperers', who hold private conversations, which while they could be related to the subject, are distracting. *Solution:* do not embarrass them. Direct some point to one of them by name, ask an easy question. Or repeat the last point and ask for comments.

■ The 'inarticulate'. Has the ideas, but can't put them across. *Solution:* say, 'Let me repeat that …' (then put it in better language).

- ■ The 'mistaken', who is clearly wrong. *Solution:* say, 'That's one way of looking at it, but how can we reconcile that with ...?' (state the correct point).
- ■ The 'silent'. Could be shy, bored, indifferent, insecure, or just might learn best by listening. *Solution:* depends on what is causing the silence. If bored or indifferent, try asking a provocative question, one you think might interest them. If shy, complement them when they do say something, and then ask direct questions from time to time to draw them in.

Even if these problem situations do not occur, we should remember to:

- ■ *Keep discussion on track*. If the group has got off track, say, 'We've had some very interesting thoughts here, but let's see if we can't get an answer to our original question', or ask follow-up questions which call for an answer leading back to the topic.
- ■ *Prevent discussion trailing into silence*. If just one person is off the track, ask him how his point contributes to the topic under discussion. If it doesn't, he'll probably drop it. Stimulate by asking follow-up questions like: 'Why?', 'What is your experience on that, John?', 'Will you give us an example?', 'Why will it work?' and, 'Is there anything else we can do to make it work?'
- ■ *Keep an eye on individuals*. Whenever you can, remember or note who says what, when they make a good point, or have to be put down. For instance, if time demands discussion has to be cut on one topic, cutting off someone anxious to make a comment, make sure that they become an early participant when the next discussion takes place.

And that, as you should probably rarely say on a training session, is all there is to it.

It is not *everything*, of course, but we have reviewed some of the key issues; besides, it is a broad topic. If you run these kinds of session and are conscious of how you go about it, and how it is received, you will spend a lifetime fine-tuning what you do. Not only does what you do improve with practice, but there is also no 'right' way. You have to do it in your own style and adapt, at least to some degree, meeting by meeting and group by group.

Whatever you do, creating and handling participation will always be a vital element, indeed a key influence on how the whole event goes. You cannot really have too much participation; but the content must be allowed to shine through, and participation must be there for specific reasons. It must support the proceedings rather than becoming an end in itself. There is a danger that the reflex can become one of, 'If in doubt, get them to do something', reminiscent of the old story about how many trainers it takes to change a light bulb. Answer: none. They simply assemble two syndicates, one to get the old bulb out, the other to put the new one in.

However, if you are well prepared, start the session off well, work at putting your message over clearly, and *involve people*, using the group to help the group and yourself, then you will find you are genuinely helping people to learn.

Just one more thing. *Always* have the last word. Right at the end when you close the session the sequence is not: summary, any final questions, close. It is: indication of the end, any last questions, summary and close. It is the same principle that says you should never finish a meeting with the ubiquitous 'Any Other Business', but send people away on a high note. Within the summary and close, a word of thanks for the participants' input may well be appropriate.

Rather like the opening remarks, closing remarks need to be well prepared. A summary should be just that. A closing remark may be:

A question                  'We started with a question, let's end with another.'

| | |
|---|---|
| A quotation or saying | 'A picture's worth a thousand words, they say – one final slide to summarize.' |
| A story | 'Let me tell you a brief story which illustrates ...'. |
| A summary | 'There are three key points to bear in mind as we close. First ...'. |
| An alternative | 'Right, so you can either opt for ... or ...'. |
| A call for action | '... and I suggest we start right now.' |

Some of these can be used in combination, and you may well be able to think of others.

And remember: *ending on time*, or even with a little time in hand, is even more important than starting on time.

So, bearing everything covered so far in mind, your next training session is going to be the best you've ever done. No? Well, you could read the material in this book again (bearing in mind repetition and retention), prepare carefully, and *then* the next session you run will be the best ever. And, more important, it will really 'help people to learn'.

But even when all has apparently gone well there is something else to consider. In the next and final chapter we consider what happens *after* the session.

## Answers from page 105

S – O T T F F S (One Two Three Four Five Six)
F goes above the line, as do all those letters made up of straight lines: ones with curves are below the line.

# 8

# Assessing ongoing effectiveness

Add value or get out.

*Lord Sheppard*

You want training to be successful, effective. Sometimes a session or a course may end with a round of applause. It's nice, but perhaps it does not measure the right thing. The session may have passed the time, been entertaining even, but given the time, effort and money that can go into development, there is clearly a need to make sure that what is done is truly worthwhile and will affect the future.

Feedback is more than a reassurance of this; it provides an opportunity to fine-tune the activities and methods used. It influences future performance. This may be simple, for example good feedback can produce a resolve to repeat a session, perhaps for others. Or it may be more complex, in the sense that a programme can be gradually adapted and improved to better reflect conditions as they change. Feedback can also assist with longer-term, and sometimes organization-wide, developments and benefit a wider group.

Clearly there is also a prime need to see whether development activities bring changes in the people undertaking them. We want to know their reaction to them, and whether their knowledge, skills, attitudes and behaviour change.

There are various ways in which the results of development can be monitored. These are not mutually exclusive; you may usefully use a combination of different methods depending on circumstances. The intention should be twofold, to 1) do the minimum that will produce the information needed, rather than allow an explosion of information to produce a glut of facts way beyond what is actually useful; 2) make the acquisition of the feedback straightforward. Systems, policy or people can sometimes have the reverse effect – recalling the story of the hospital patient who had to telephone the hospital posing as a relative to discover how their state of health was viewed! There are several possible methods, discussed below.

# Informal monitoring

Staff may sometimes complain that they never, or rarely, see their managers (others may, of course, complain they see them too much!) But if management time is skimped – no doubt because of other, seemingly more important pressures – then the first kind of contact to go will be ones linked to 'inessentials' such as development. After all, it is rationalized, operational matters must continue and be given priority.

The realities here can dilute the manager/staff relationship, inhibit motivation, and give rise to the sort of culture characterized by the remark, 'The only time I see my manager is if something has gone wrong.' So, time must be found for some meetings and for discussion about developmental matters.

Further, this should be on a regular basis, certainly rather than being the sort of thing that only occurs 'when time permits', and applied across all staff, rather than seeming to favour a few. (This may be necessary sometimes; however, one thing to avoid is spending most of your available time with any poor performers. While their situation may well need addressing, the greatest increase in performance can come from development activity applied to those already doing fine.)

Informal monitoring can take many forms, including for instance:

▓ meetings scheduled through the year to follow up annual appraisal sessions;
▓ fact-finding sessions to help plan future development activities;
▓ briefings about forthcoming training;
▓ debriefing after a course has been attended (or other training completed);
▓ counselling or monitoring of projects linked to training, either informal projects arranged between manager and staff or projects from sandwich courses (ie, two course sessions linked with a project);
▓ items on the agenda of other (perhaps departmental) meetings addressing particular aspects of development;
▓ informal (and perhaps unstructured) meetings – as you pass on the stairs or chat over a sandwich.

There are more formal elements to some of these that link with comments under the headings that follow.

Two things will add power to this kind of activity. First, *a continuing dialogue*, which implies the manager must make efforts to commit things to memory, or better still make a note, so that one exchange can be linked to the next, which will prove more effective than an ad hoc approach. Second always *using two-way dialogue*: it will work better if people feel able to be involved, consulted and indeed feel that the whole process is something from which you intend them to gain.

The cumulative effect of this sort of activity should not be underestimated, nor should the impact of the simplest things. I have mentioned (page 49) my own case when I began writing – hesitatingly and inexpertly – for publication, and mentoring kick-started and developed the process. This helped disproportionately, both immediately and by supplying ways of remembering key things and thus developing the right habits. It was here, I think, in the interests of not unnecessarily overusing long words that I first heard what is now one of my favourite quotations, from Mark Twain who said, 'I never write the word "metropolis" if I get paid the same to write the word "city".'

From the management perspective, continuity of this sort of process needs a little thought, but it needs no major commitment of time or effort.

Forgive what may seem like returning to a digression, but I believe describing my situation helps make the point that the little things are as important as the big; more so in some ways as there is a more realistic prospect of finding opportunity and time for them. Before long doing so can become a habit for any manager and the whole process gains momentum. In my case, well over 50 books later, I know just how useful this kind of low-key input can be.

A final word to stress here is communication. You will have noticed that much that has now been said about what needs to be done in monitoring progress, indeed about getting the most from development, is – in one way or another – communication. Although it cannot literally be true, it is worth saying that a moral here is that you cannot communicate too much about development. Planning and managing to communicate sufficiently and in the right way is crucial, and well worth striving towards.

As we move on, mention of communication will reoccur, so no apology for that.

# Testing training effectiveness

With certain kinds of training, some measurement of it is essentially straightforward. This is very much the case when training is directed primarily at imparting knowledge. You want to know how much has 'stuck'. So, you can use a simple test.

This may be written or verbal, or involve various computer technologies that can take the user through a series of test questions, scoring and reinforcing knowledge in the event of error as they go.

Applications here range widely, but include matters such as product knowledge, numerical or procedural process, keyboard or language skills and many more. Time spent here can be very useful. Knowing a test is coming may concentrate the mind of trainees and, at worst, it can pick up a complete lack of aptitude at an early stage before too much time and money are spent.

## Seeing for yourself

Sometimes the nature of the task, the development and the individual means that there is a need to both observe and to get involved to correct anything necessary to improve or extend performance. A public manifestation of this is when we telephone a company and hear an announcement made telling us that, 'some calls may be recorded'. Sometimes, for example in the insurance industry, this is for legal reasons, but training is a prime reason too.

The essence of the activity here is that you observe something happening and then, if necessary, act on it either at once or later. This is not, however, just a question of negative critique (certainly not of threats) and demanding that things are done differently. Nor does it just describe the 'right way' and suggest people get on with it.

The process should be motivational – this is something that should be kept in mind throughout – and dealt with sensitively and systematically. This extends what has been said regarding on-the-job development and the classic stages, essentially: telling, showing, prompting practice, assessing, coaching and follow-up discussions such as agreeing further action. The details were set out in Chapter 4 and will not be re-stated here. Consider the last stage for a moment, however: the agreement of follow-up. What needs to happen next will vary. It may be little or nothing. It could be that such a session forms the start (or is already a part of) an ongoing series of developmental inputs, or that something like a note in the diary, the individual's file or your own needs to be made. The reliability of agreed follow-up taking place is very motivational. Conversely, saying, 'Let's have a brief word about that next week,' and then forgetting is a waste – make notes.

The procedure described here will need to be considered in the light of the experience of the trainee. The principles described apply to first time briefing and, with a less 'from scratch' approach, to tasks which have to be regularly checked.

It is also worth mentioning the place where this sort of session is conducted. It may be informal, straightforward and cause no problem to conduct it at the trainee's desk, even if the workstation is in an open plan area. Or it might be better if such a session were more private. Additionally, some jobs and tasks do not take place in the workplace and yet still have to be observed and worked on in this kind of way. A classic example of this is the field sales job. A sales manager should regularly accompany members of his or her sales team, sitting in on meetings for evaluation purposes and discussing them later – at what is, in sales, called a 'kerbside conference' because it often takes place in the car used to get from call to call. Sometimes the nature of the sales process means that this observation can even be done without the customer's knowledge, as in publishing where many retail calls are conducted out in a book-shop and a manager can browse nearby and listen.

Judgement is needed regarding place, as a trainee feeling awkward (because his or her colleagues can hear, for instance) will be less likely to concentrate. A manager constantly interrupted by other things will find the same.

# Course assessment

Here we look at the measurement associated with training courses of whatever sort: these include attendance on public programmes, courses held in-house (and conducted either by training staff, an outside training consultant – or you), even the use of training packages.

Sometimes courses may be used for motivational or other reasons, most often we want to know that they have met their objectives and are likely to have some positive effect on action. Measurement may take a little time, though not an unreasonable amount and only a small percentage of the actual training time. It can involve several stages (some of these might be omitted, or dealt with more simply, but any decisions to do so should be made carefully). So, consider the following.

## A pre-course briefing

This may include a discussion about the choice of course (or the choice to do some training), and should ensure that both manager and trainee are agreed on why attendance is desirable and what should be got from it. It may take an overall view or go into some detail, for example creating a checklist of points that should be raised on the course. (As a trainer I like nothing better than when people attend courses with a clear idea of how they hope to benefit.)

## An evaluation form

At most courses an evaluation form will be used. This may be for the benefit of the trainer or organizer, but a copy may be usefully retained or an organization may have its own form, designed to its requirements and issued to those attending

**The Chartered Institute of Marketing**

Course Code:

## Your Assessment

Name: _____ Company: _____ Post Code: _____

Job Title: _____ Course: _____

My Email Address: (Please print clearly) _____
NB. This would only be used to email CIM information. We do not share our database with 3rd parties.
If you wish **not** to receive information in this way please opt out by marking the box ☐

*Please mark your answers like this:* ⊢ *Please do not tick.*

| Who made the decision for you to attend this course? | [ ] Myself | [ ] My Manager | [ ] Training Dept |
|---|---|---|---|

**Expectations:**      V Satisfied ⟵————⟶ V Dissat
Are you satisfied that the **course objectives were as described in the literature?** [ ] [ ] [ ] [ ] [ ]
To what extent are you satisfied that the **course objectives were met?** [ ] [ ] [ ] [ ] [ ]

**Delivery:**      Excellent ⟵————⟶ V Poor
How would you evaluate the overall **content?** [ ] [ ] [ ] [ ] [ ]
How would you evaluate the overall **structure?** [ ] [ ] [ ] [ ] [ ]
Did you have enough opportunity to ask questions? [ ] [ ] [ ] [ ] [ ]
Did the presenter establish a good **rapport?** [ ] [ ] [ ] [ ] [ ]

**Materials:**      Excellent ⟵————⟶ V Poor
Please rate the quality of the **visual presentation** [ ] [ ] [ ] [ ] [ ]
Please rate the quality of the **handouts** [ ] [ ] [ ] [ ] [ ]

**Administration:**      Excellent ⟵————⟶ V Poor
How well did we handle your booking? [ ] [ ] [ ] [ ] [ ]
How well were you looked after during the course? [ ] [ ] [ ] [ ] [ ]
How satisfied were you with the catering? [ ] [ ] [ ] [ ] [ ]

**Overall:**      Excellent ⟵————⟶ V Poor
How would you evaluate the course **overall?** [ ] [ ] [ ] [ ] [ ]
Would you **recommend** the course to others?    YES [ ] [ ] NO

**Topic Comments:**
Should any other topics have been included or received **greater emphasis?**
Should any of the topics have been omitted or received **less emphasis?**

**Further Comments:** We are constantly improving our training programmes. Please tell us what you really think.

(Continue overleaf if necessary)

**Training Providers:**
Which other training providers does your company use? _____
     V Well ⟵————⟶ Poorly
How does CIM compare? _____ [ ] [ ] [ ] [ ] [ ]

**MY further training needs:**
Please contact me on Tel. No _____ as I would like to attend another CIM Course.

**My COMPANY'S further training needs:**
Please contact _____ who is my company's training contact, on Tel No _____
to arrange to have this or another event tailored to my company's requirements.

Thank you for being a delegate on this course. We look forward to welcoming you again.

CIMAHOUS HOUS CIMAHOUS    FeedBack Tel: 01628 784423    24 Mar 04

**Figure 8.1** *Example of course assessment form*

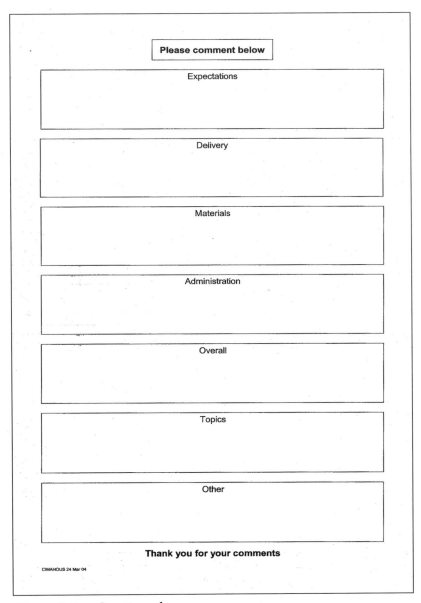

**Figure 8.1** *Continued*

public seminars, for example. These are useful in providing an immediate impression of the course, its content and form.

Figure 8.1 provides a good example. It is used by the Chartered Institute of Marketing (with which I am involved), but it a good clear form and is tried and tested on large numbers of delegates. Thanks to them for permission to reproduce it here.

# A post-course debriefing

The fact that a form exists should not blind you to the merits of sitting down with someone on his or her return from training. Such a session is best planned, and even scheduled, before attendance takes place. The completed form may act as an agenda or checklist for a discussion and the onus then is likely to be on the future – for example, what action or further training will follow. Sometimes further documentation may be useful, perhaps to put something on file as a guide to future users of the same programme.

# Longer-term review

It may also be worth considering a longer-term review. First, many courses seem good in the immediate aftermath: it was interesting, fun and a few days away from the office – but what matters most is the way behaviour is changed in the future. Secondly, the review can link to specific projects and with the actual job. For example, people attending a report-writing course may be asked to write a report for discussion with their manager or, better still, use the next one they have to write as a basis of discussion designed to extend the thinking started on the training and to consider how useful it has been. Such longer-term reviews may involve meetings and further evaluation forms or reports.

## The link to appraisal

Ultimately individual training inputs may come up for discussion at the next formal job appraisal. As has been mentioned elsewhere, development is a prime consideration in such sessions.

Not least, the whole sequence described here bestows importance on training as a process, and on the particular development that is taking place. It is thus motivational for the individual concerned, as well as providing feedback and a basis for action for both manager and staff. Incidentally, it is worth noting that members of your staff have probably come across the advice that this should be done. They may well expect it, and think less well of an employer who does not do it.

# Annual job appraisal

As this has been commented on earlier in the review, no great detail is required here. Suffice to say that this is relevant here as the annual culmination of all the checks and discussions held during the year. It provides an opportunity for you to review the net result of all training and development undertaken during the year for each individual member of your team. It provides a good moment to comment on the most recent activity and, of course, to discuss the continuation of what is usually an ongoing process.

# The ultimate alternative

Whatever training and development you undertake, and whatever monitoring of results may follow it, there is no absolute certainty that everything will work. Occasionally it becomes clear that an individual will never make the grade. This may be for all sorts of reasons: poor selection, lack of motivation, sheer inability – whatever.

Sometimes the reason provides useful feedback; for example, poor selection might hold a moral for future recruitment which, handled differently, might produce better candidates. On other occasions it is simply a fact of life – not everyone can do everything. It may also be a side-effect of recent technology, with someone moved from, say, a bank branch customer service role to one of the call centres that now substitute for much of that activity, finding that they cannot cope with the computer systems involved.

Given poor – unacceptable – performance the choices open to you are few. You can:

■   put up with it (which is not to be recommended);
■   apply some sort of remedial action (classically development or training, though it might be that motivation needs boosting);
■   change procedures (maybe what is being asked is unreasonable, few could perform acceptably and only new approaches or methods will ensure the required performance);
■   terminate the employment of the person concerned (or move them elsewhere).

The rules here are simple. Having checked things like procedures and motivation, development must be provided if the problem is a skill shortfall of some sort. If appropriate – even sustained – development is given a fair chance and performance is still not improving then the only option may be to fire someone. This is not something to be done lightly, and is unpleasant for you, the employee and those around you. But when push comes to shove it may have to be done. No one likes it if a team carries passengers, least of all when others must make up the shortfall. Ultimately your job is to produce results and problems of under-performance must be tackled.

Few (no?) things that are difficult become easier if delayed. It is all too easy, given the way it is usually viewed, to put off this sort of ultimate action, rationalizing and waiting for improvement that, in all honesty, is not actually on the cards. Once the point has been reached where the reason for poor performance is clearly established, and if training is indicated this has been given a fair chance, then swift action is usually best. This can be tempered with a benevolent policy about severance arrangements, and this is something many organizations favour for motivational and public relations reasons. Remember too the legal aspects of this situation (employment legislation is complex, ever-changing and the details matter, even if they are beyond the brief here).

That said, let's be positive and end by suggesting that training can more usually cure problems that may occur. Indeed improved performance potential may provide opportunities for people to progress far beyond their original post, or indeed intention; and for the organization to benefit from their career progress.

# Afterword

When you're through changing, you're through.
Change is a process, not a goal; a journey not
a destination.

*Robert Kriegal and David Brant*

Another title I have written for this series is *Successful Time Management*. That topic is relevant here. Many managers do less to advise, coach and develop their people than they might, than is necessary and often than they would like. The most common reason for this is stated as being 'lack of time'. Yet doing so is surely a priority. Time spent to ensure that things are done properly, are done well – indeed that excellent performance is made more likely – is time well spent. Doing so should not be a chore, it should not be skimped and the time equation here is a positive one: when managers spend time on development, results can be improved in a way that goes far beyond what managers can achieve just by doing more themselves.

Of course, it helps to be well organized, to put yourself in a position to spend some appropriate time on development, but the motivation for this should be high. Indeed, any managers who skimp their people development responsibilities risk giving themselves and their department or organization a serious handicap. This may act, day by day, to dilute the efficiency and effectiveness of operations and, at worst, may end as the cause of failure to produce the planned results.

Consider the advantages of a positive initiative in this area. By imparting knowledge, developing skills and changing attitudes, successful training and development can:

■ act as a significant motivator (affecting such factors as staff retention);
■ change and improve performance short term;
■ ensure long-term operational excellence is maintained;
■ keep people and organizations ahead of external and internal changes;
■ create differentiation in the marketplace through the way people interact externally.

There is, as with so much in management, no magic formula to guarantee instant success. It needs a systematic approach, it needs planning and it needs care in execution. It can – and must – utilize an increasingly wide and disparate range of development methods. The simplest action may, in either the short or long term, be as useful and as significant in its results as something more complex.

If there is anything that comes near to a magic formula, or which at least offers a clue to how to proceed overall, it is continuity. The way ahead is to maintain a continuing focus on development. This involves:

■ planning ahead and anticipating events (as far as possible);
■ reacting accurately when surprises occur (as they will);
■ taking action (whether what is done is major or minor) progressively;
■ letting the cumulative effect of different things build up;
■ adopting a broad view of the people and the organization.

In this way, the positive effect of development gradually builds. It will then add power to operations and give satisfaction to those who participate in it. It is a process that never ends. Adopting the attitude that 'even the best performance can be improved' is a sound one; something John Wooden said: 'It's what you learn after you know it all that counts', makes the point. And ultimately the time and effort any developmental activity takes will be reflected in the ongoing results that people are able to achieve.

Your people may, rightly, be given the credit for what they achieve; you may take credit for the fact that you have put in place an initiative taking them in the right direction and enabling them to maximize their performance.

# Other titles in the Kogan Page Creating Success series

*Be Positive*, 2nd edition, by Phil Clements
*Better Business Writing* by Timothy R V Foster
*Dealing With Difficult People* by Roy Lilley
*Develop Your Assertiveness*, 2nd edition, by Sue Bishop
*Develop Your NLP Skills*, 3rd edition, by Andrew Bradbury
*The Effective Leader* by Rupert Eales-White
*How to Manage Meetings* by Alan Barker
*How to Motivate People*, 2nd edition, by Patrick Forsyth
*How to Negotiate Effectively* by David Oliver
*How to Understand Business Finance* by Bob Cinnamon and
   Brian Helweg-Larsen
*How to Write a Business Plan*, 2nd edition, by Brian Finch
*How to Write a Marketing Plan*, 3rd edition, by John
   Westwood
*How to Write Reports and Proposals*, 2nd edition, by Patrick
   Forsyth
*Improve Your Communication Skills*, 2nd edition by Alan
   Barker
*Organise Yourself*, 2nd edition, by John Caunt
*Successful Presentation Skills*, 3rd edition, by Andrew
   Bradbury
*Successful Project Management*, 2nd edition, by Trevor Young
*Successful Time Management* by Patrick Forsyth
*Taking Minutes of Meetings*, 2nd edition, by Joanna Gutmann
*Understanding Brands* by Peter Cheverton

The above titles are available from all good bookshops. For further information on these and other Kogan Page titles, or to order online, visit the Kogan Page website at
**www.kogan-page.co.uk**

# The *Creating Success* series

Published in association with **THE SUNDAY TIMES**

ISBN: 978 0 7494 4547 8
Paperback 2006

ISBN: 978 0 7494 4918 6
Paperback 2007

ISBN: 978 0 7494 4919 3
Paperback 2007

ISBN: 978 0 7494 4866 0
Paperback 2007

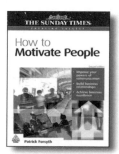

ISBN: 978 0 7494 4551 5
Paperback 2006

ISBN: 978 0 7494 4668 0
Paperback 2006

Order now at www.kogan-page.co.uk